Pythagoras

D1649582

By the same author

Poetry
Walking Under Water
Tenants of the House
Poems, Golders Green
A Small Desperation
Selected Poems
Funland and Other Poems
Collected Poems 1948-1976

Plays
Three Questor Plays
The Dogs of Pavlov

Prose
Ash on a Young Man's Sleeve
O. Jones, O. Jones
A Poet in the Family

Dannie Abse

PYTHAGORAS

Hutchinson of London

Hutchinson & Co. (Publishers) Ltd
3 Fitzroy Square, London W1P 6JD

London Melbourne Sydney Auckland
Wellington Johannesburg and agencies
throughout the world

First published 1979

© Dannie Abse 1979

Funland first published 1973
© Dannie Abse 1973

Applications for performances of
Pythagoras should be addressed to The
International Copyright Bureau Ltd,
Suite 8D and E, 26 Charing Cross
Road, London WC2

Set in Linotype Century

Printed in Great Britain by
The Anchor Press Ltd
Tiptree, Essex.

British Library Cataloguing in Publication data

Abse, Dannie
  Pythagoras.
  I. Title
  822'.9'14   PR6001.B7P/

ISBN 0 09 139431 7

Contents

Introduction   9
Pythagoras   15
Funland   83

Introduction

Introduction

Though not actually stoned on sight, the poet in the British theatre now more than ever is viewed with deep suspicion. Understandably so. For what inveterate theatregoer has not had to endure, in the name of poetry drama, long passages of humourless, ornamental language that obstructed rather than advanced both the characterization of the protagonists and the dynamics (such as they were) of the play itself? Who, on such occasions, has not wished for good plain prose and the verisimilitude of ordinary conversation?

Unlike Keats or Browning or Tennyson or other nineteenth-century poets who, in writing for the theatre, misguidedly borrowed the conventions of Elizabethan metrics, some later poets have invented a more distinctive personal idiom. Yet, as dramatists, they too have largely failed. Even Yeats's plays 'need to be seen as poetry literally projected on the stage',[1] while T. S. Eliot remarked percipiently of his own later dramas, 'I laid down for myself the ascetic rule to avoid poetry which could not stand the test of strict dramatic utility: with such success, indeed, that it is perhaps an open question whether there is any poetry in the plays at all.'[2]

When I was a medical student in 1947, I completed a verse drama and sent it to T. S. Eliot who commended it for being 'as much for the stage as for the study'. He was too kind: it was neither for stage nor for study

---

[1] *Sailing into the Unknown*, M. L. Rosenthal (O. U. P. 1978), p. 135
[2] *On Poetry and Poets*, T. S. Eliot (Faber, 1952), p. 83

9

and should have remained in the secrecy of a dark drawer. Ten years or so later, when I finished another play, 'House of Cowards',[3] poetry drama as a distinctive category of theatre, and as practised by T. S. Eliot, Christopher Fry, and Ronald Duncan, was discredited. The fashion had passed – no longer were such plays staged in or off Shaftesbury Avenue – and by now, in any case, I had developed my own notions about diction in the theatre. I still thought of 'House of Cowards' as a mutated poetry play – indeed it had begun life as a poem, 'The Meeting',[4] but in offering it for production I did not own up to it being such and even when subsequently it won the Charles Henry Foyle Award and attendant publicity followed I did not advertise its genesis. Given the prejudice in the theatre, then as now, against poets and poetry I think in retrospect I was wise not to be altogether open about the matter.

Wise or not, I shall own up here to the origins of 'Pythagoras'. For like 'House of Cowards' it too sprang out of a long poem, one this time called 'Funland'. And now, fashion or no fashion, I am content if any reader or any playgoer should discover 'Pythagoras' to be the work of a poet in the theatre whether that judgement be a compliment or a curse.

When 'Funland' (see appendix) was broadcast on Radio 3 I was asked to introduce the poem. It may be of some small interest if I print the prolegomenon to that BBC broadcast here. ' "Funland" ', I remarked – it was in 1971 – ' "Funland" is the longest poem that I have written. When I began it I had no thought of writing a long poem in nine parts – which is the form that "Funland" now takes. But when I completed Section One, "The Superintendent", I realized that the poem was not finished and that I could best continue it by

---

[3] *Plays of the Year 23*, Ed. by J. C. Trewin (Elek 1962)
[4] *Collected Poems 1948-1976*, Dannie Abse (Hutchinson 1977) p. 41–3.

inventing allied scenes with the same décor and with the same stylistic tone as "The Superintendent". . . .'

There were other starting points. During the making of the poem various references came to mind. For instance, once, many years ago in conversation, the novelist, Elias Canetti said to me, 'The man suffering from paranoia is correct. Someone *is* standing behind that door pumping invisible gas through the keyhole. For we are dying, right now, a little every minute.'

I thought of Canetti's remark several times while working on 'Funland' and also how the insane startle us with their metaphors and with their occasional searing truths. I thought, too, of how once Freud had remarked to Wilhelm Reich that 'the whole of humanity is my patient'.[5] Again I recalled T. S. Eliot's lines from 'East Coker':

The whole earth is our hospital
Endowed by the ruined millionaire.

My experience of human irrationality, the discovery of it in my own behaviour and in others, as I encounter it in my personal life and in my medical practice, as I am affected by it in the absurdity of public political action, as indeed I am threatened by it in the clash of public powers, makes me feel sometimes, as I'm sure it does others, that the earth is no ordinary hospital but a lunatic asylum whose inmates live out suffering lives of black comedy.

Technically (in 'Funland') I have attempted to use surrealistic images and effects with humour. For if a long poem is to be sad then perhaps there must be points in it when the reader should laugh. What else to say? I could talk, I suppose, about the contemporary white coat of Medicine and the old purple cloak of charismatic Mesmer – their relationship and opposition to each other. But I would rather not. Too much that

---

[5] *Reich speaks of Freud*, Ed. Higgins and Raphael (Noonday Press 1967), p. 77

I would say would be 'a rationalization after the event'. In writing poetry, often I am copying something that is invisible and only afterwards can I see what my model was. So I shall just read you the poem, 'Funland'."

Not long after the broadcast of 'Funland' I accepted an invitation to go along to the New College of Speech and Drama at Pavlova House where they were presenting an evening of dramatic poetry. The students had worked from a BBC script of 'Funland' and had made their own dramatization of the poem much to my surprise, embarrassment and interest. I did not know it then but that student production was the next step towards 'Pythagoras' for it gave me the idea that 'Funland' could be dramatized and perhaps in a more radical way than the New College students had envisaged.

This new dramatization of 'Funland' was presented at the Questors Theatre New Plays Festival of 1975. It was far from being a success. I needed to start again – to forget the actual lines of the poem 'Funland' but not the active characters in the poem. Garry O'Connor reviewing my free dramatization of 'Funland' in the *Financial Times* suggested the character of Pythagoras could be developed in an exciting way, and he referred to Thomas Mann's *'Mario and the Magician'*. I was, in any case, becoming more and more interested in the personality of those who are thought by others, rightly or wrongly, to own peculiar, even mysterious powers. So I took Mr O'Connor's advice: I re-read the Mann story, I re-remembered my own experience as a medical student and as a visitor to mental hospitals, and keeping in mind Coleridge's dictum that comedy is the blossom of the nettle, wrote 'Pythagoras'.

Pythagoras

'Pythagoras' was first produced at the Birmingham Repertory Theatre on 22 September 1976. The cast was as follows:

Pythagoras   Roger Sloman
Charlie   Peter Gordon
Dr Robert Aquillus   John Sterland
Nurse Grey   Susan Brown
Marian Cunningham   Barbara Flynn
Ellen   Helen Horton
Biddy Morgan   Annette Badland
Mr X   Colin Kaye
Ken Kennedy   Colin Higgins
Arthur Haines   Graham Seed
Dr Bruce Green   Robert Benfield

Directed by Peter Farago

Act One

Scene One

The superintendent's office. *On stage right is a desk with in-trays, blotting paper, telephone: on stage left is a white coat on a coat-hanger. Apart from usual office furniture there is a covered parrot's cage. As the lights come up,* **Pythagoras Smith,** *a tall white-faced man just under forty, is bringing up a conductor's baton over his head. As he does so, a twangy musical note becomes louder. When he slowly brings down the baton the lights lower and the twangy note softens. In short, it would appear that* **Pythagoras** *with his baton is controlling the degree of lighting on the stage and the loudness of the curious music. Now, as the music and lights become more powerful,* **Pythagoras** *looks stern.*

Pythagoras: [*shouting*] Cease! Stop! Stop, I say!

[*Lights become fixed. Music ceases.* **Pythagoras,** *delighted with his own power, smiles briefly at the audience. This time, as he brings down the baton, lights go down slowly, but the musical note begins and becomes louder and is loudest when stage is dark*]

Pythagoras: [*above music*] Now again. C'mon, c'mon. That's it.

[*As lights come on slowly and brighten, the music becomes softer and finally ceases.*]

15

Pythagoras: Ha, ha, ha, very good, ha, ha, ha. I'm on form.

[*Enter* **Charlie**, *a short middle-aged man who is evidently surprised to see* **Pythagoras**]

Charlie: What's the joke, Pythagoras?

Pythagoras: Ha, ha, ha. Mornin', Charlie.

Charlie: What are you doin' in Dr Aquillus's office?

Pythagoras: What are *you* doing in Dr Aquillus's office?

Charlie: That a conductor's baton?

Pythagoras: Listen, Charlie, when I bring this cane down slowly the light will fade and you'll hear a very strange unusual note.

Charlie: Go on.

[**Pythagoras** *brings down baton slowly. Nothing happens. No change of light nor any sound, but* **Pythagoras** *seems pleased*]

Pythagoras: Bravo, now cease! Stop, I say. Ha, ha, ha. What do you think of that? The music of the spheres. I'll tell you the secret of how to make magic, Charlie.

Charlie: Mmm?

[*Pause*]

Pythagoras: Think blue, say green. And squeeze apple-pips from a tangerine. Ha, ha, ha.

Charlie: Music of the spheres, my foot. Like I said to Dr Aquillus, you're just a second-class stage magician with a paid-up Equity card now in the bin with the rest of us.

Pythagoras: [*lifting baton*] Now I'll restore the sunlight. It'll be a beautiful June morning again. [*Baton now over his head*] What do you think of that, eh?

Charlie: No wonder you never made the Palladium.

Pythagoras: The speed of light deceives the eye.

Charlie: You could have fooled me!

Pythagoras: If you'd studied Anaximander, read the accounts of Babylonian astronomy and Egyptian mensuration you too would have heard the music of the spheres. And I could teach even *you* how to intensify light and delete it.

Charlie: Just because you think you've been reincarnated –

Pythagoras: My disciples used to say there were three kinds of rational creatures: gods, men, and those such as me, Pythagoras, first philosopher, astronomer, mathematician and magician.

Charlie: [*mockingly*] I know all about you, mate. Put on the right shoe first, wash the left foot first. No meat, no fish, no beans.

[**Charlie** *takes baton from* **Pythagoras**]

Pythagoras: [*with dignity*] That's only partly true. I don't know where you got hold of that. But even the ancient sources that scholars use are unreliable. They listen to a little gossip in a great silence. My life story, Charlie, is a scratch on a worn stone of the sixth century BC. Yes, I – be careful with my magic cane. Don't bend it! Like the sceptre of Zeus, it's made of cypress wood.

Charlie: [*sneering*] Magic cane? Ha, ha, ha, it's from Woolworth's. Music of the stars. Ker-rist.

Pythagoras: You be careful. Careful. Magic is a primitive form of applied science and like science it gives you power.

Charlie: You call this bit of wood, this baton, magic! You're over the top, old fella. It's time you heard the truth, time –

Pythagoras: [*annoyed*] My magic cane will stick to your hand. It's stuck to your hand.

17

Charlie: What?

Pythagoras: Throw it on the floor, you can't, you can't.

Charlie: Course I can, don't be daft.

Pythagoras: You can't get rid of it. Try it, go on, ha, ha, ha.

[**Charlie** *tries to throw cane on to the floor, but it won't leave his hand.* **Pythagoras** *is laughing*]

Charlie: [*mumbling*] Damn stick. It's got glue on it.

Pythagoras: Ha, ha, ha.

Charlie: [*over*] Dr Aquillus said you mustn't hypnotize any of us. He expressly said hypnotism verboten.

Pythagoras: Are you hypnotized?

Charlie: Course not.

Pythagoras: What's the temperature of that *magic* cane?

Charlie: Temperature?

Pythagoras: Don't you feel its starlike magnetic heat?

Charlie: It *is* lukewarm.

Pythagoras: It's warming up. It's getting hotter and you can't let go.

Charlie: It is getting hotter. Ouch, ouch.

Pythagoras: It's hotter still.

Charlie: Ouch, ouch! [*yells*] Aw. Crikey.

[**Charlie** *jumps up and down shouting*]

Pythagoras: OK. OK. Don't make such a shindy.

Charlie: Aw, aw. I'm burning. *Burning.*

Pythagoras: It's getting cooler. It's cooling.

Charlie: Aw. Ouch. Ah.

Pythagoras: Definitely cooling. When it gets cold you'll be able to drop it on the floor.

Charlie: Yes, ah, aw, yes. Aaah.

[**Charlie** *drops cane. He looks at his hand*]

I'll roast you one day, Pythagoras. Look at my hand. Scalded.

[*Sound of a distant clock striking nine*]

Pythagoras: Dr Aquillus will be here soon. We better beat it.

Charlie: I don't like Aquillus. He's stingy. Gives away nothing.

Pythagoras: Right. He only smiles in millimetres. He resembles Polycrates.

Charlie: Poly . . . who?

Pythagoras: Polycrates, tyrant of Samos, where I was born two and a half thousand years ago. Do you know what Polycrates valued most?

Charlie: Your gifts?

Pythagoras: His signet ring. I used to say, 'Friendship is Equality, Polycrates'. But he wouldn't listen. He was only interested in building the temple of Hera and constructing the great seawalls of the harbour. And a tunnel nearly a mile long to bring –

[**Pythagoras** *suddenly and quickly exits left. He has heard the approach of the superintendent,* **Dr Aquillus***, who enters right.* **Dr Robert Aquillus** *is a kindly, absent-minded stooping man nearing retiring age.* **Charlie** *picks up baton*]

Charlie: Pythagoras, you've left your –

Aquillus: What are you doing here?

Charlie: Mornin', doctor. Come here to show you my right hand, Dr Aquillus.

Aquillus: Can't play now, Charlie. I haven't had breakfast yet.

Charlie: It's scalded.

Aquillus: What is?

[*Enter* **Nurse Grey** *with breakfast tray*]

Nurse: Good morning, Dr Aquillus. Beautiful morning, Charlie.

Charlie: This conductor's baton here. It got very hot.

Nurse: Dr Aquillus has a busy day today, Charlie. The concert tonight. The madrigals to rehearse and so on. Do get *your* breakfast before the others eat it.

Aquillus: What time are the students coming from Westminster Hospital?

Nurse: Ten-thirty.

Charlie: [*loud*] Look at my hand. I bloody well order you to look at my hand. My right hand.

[**Charlie** *with left hand throws baton high into the air. It falls on to the floor*]

Aquillus: Charlie seems more than usually disturbed this morning.

Nurse: Perhaps he could be your demonstration patient.

Charlie: No, don't choose me, doctor. *Please.* Choose Pythagoras. He thinks he can hypnotize people. The students would love that. My hand's OK now, don't worry. Please don't choose me.

Aquillus: I'm not going to choose you, Charlie. Relax.

Charlie: Thank you, doctor. Good doctor. Shall I take the cover off the parrot's cage for you, doctor?

Nurse: I'll do that. You go and get your breakfast.

Charlie: Thank you, Nurse Grey. Thank you, doctor.

[*Exit* **Charlie** *bowing*]

[*At door*] I do like your signet ring, doctor.

[**Charlie** *exits.* **Nurse** *takes cover off parrot's cage.* **Dr Aquillus** *butters toast*]

Aquillus: Illness takes the mask off people. Poor Charlie.

Nurse: There you are, Polly. There you are, isn't that better? I do wish it would answer.

Aquillus: Not one word have I got out of that parrot since it came here to The Cedars. Mute. Catatonic. It's difficult to organize a meaningful therapeutic relationship with that bird, ha ha ha.

Nurse: By the way, doctor, Marian Cunningham is anxious to know what day you're discharging her.

Aquillus: [*rising*] Is she assisting Pythagoras at the concert tonight?

Nurse: Yes.

Aquillus: That might stir her up. Better leave it till this weekend is over.

Nurse: Monday then?

Aquillus: Any day next week.

[**Dr Aquillus** *stares at parrot as he stands drinking his morning tea. The* **Nurse**, *about to leave, picks up the cane but immediately drops it as if it were red-hot*]

Nurse: Ouch!

[*Startled by* **Nurse's** *loud cry* **Dr Aquillus** *simultaneously drops his saucer*]

Aquillus: What's the matter?

Nurse: [*looking at cane puzzled*] Oh, nothing. Just some static electricity.

[*Lights down to darkness and music up of 'These Foolish Things'*]

Scene Two

The common room. *The radio is playing 'These*

Foolish Things'. To the right is a large urn from which patients can take coffee or tea. Three women enter right to take their coffee. They are **Biddy**, *a fat, depressed woman in her thirties;* **Marian**, *an attractive twenty-four-year-old; and* **Ellen**, *an American middle-aged lady who turns off the radio.*

Biddy: I'm still hungry. That was a very low-caloried breakfast.

Ellen: You ate Arthur's egg besides your own. I saw you. [*pause*] To think you'll be leaving us soon, Marian. I remember your first day.

Marian: It was such a relief to be put to bed, to be looked after.

Ellen: Damn thing is they force you to get up after twenty-four hours. Go into the common room, Ellen, they said. Meet up with the others. Like a hole in the head I wanted that. I didn't wanna meet up with anybody, no Joe Blow or anybody, no sir. I need sedatives, Dr Aquillus, I said. Gimme deep sleep treatment, Bob, I said. I wanted out. Religion saved me.

Marian: [*happily*] Just think. It's over. No more group therapy. No more OT.

Ellen: I hate making baskets.

Biddy: No more set meals.

Marian: No more *regimentation*. If they'll let me I shall quit The Cedars tomorrow. Saturday's a good day to leave.

Ellen: If they give you an option leave it to the Lord's Day. Yep, the good Lord would –

[**Biddy** *yawns ostentatiously*]

You stop yawning. You should read the Bible.

Biddy: Oh Gawd, she's off.

Ellen: There's a lotta wonderful people in the Bible. It's the *greatest* book.

Marian: I feel ... so light. I feel ... confident. Just like I used to.

Ellen: Yeh. Yeh, I know, baby. [*pause*] Automation's the big thing but I believe in the Bible.

Biddy: Can't whip up any interest.

Ellen: Just think: Jesus promised paradise to a dying thief in exchange for *one* kind word. Isn't that wonderful?

Biddy: You Yanks ... so gullible. Mind you ... the story of the Virgin birth would be very interesting, in my opinion, if you happened to know the people involved personally.

Marian: Ha, ha, ha.

[*Sounds of* **Charlie** *off stage shouting,* 'Good morning, good morning, good morning.' *He enters speaking rapidly and takes very short steps. He helps himself to coffee still muttering*]

Charlie: Good morning good morning good morning good morning good morning good morning good morning. [*sits down right*]

Marian: What energy!

Biddy: You missed breakfast this morning, Charlie.

Charlie: Just finished it. Bloody awful it was, too. Toast burned. Tea stewed. Butter rancid, and I bet this coffee will taste institutional.

Biddy: Ever asked Pythagoras's opinion on the Bible?

Ellen: Pythagoras! That heathen! He's just a bum heathen who believes in the reincarnation racket.

Charlie: [*shouting*] Don't you ladies know my father was a train driver?

Marian: I bet he drove an express.

Charlie: He knew every signal between Euston and Preston. It wasn't all roses, you know. He had to look out for people throwing themselves under the engine.

Ellen: For Chris'sake.

Charlie: Dad ran over 'undreds in his time. Hundreds. Never look back, he used to say, that's the trick, son. Never look back, it only upsets you.

Marian: Never look back.

Ellen: *Never* look back.

Biddy: Never, never.

Charlie: Coming home excited, looking forward to seeing the wife again, the kids, on a windy autumn afternoon, coming home twenty-four hours early, arms full of things – I dunno – luggage, gifts, flowers. . . .

Biddy: Chrysanthemums. . . .

Charlie: . . . shutting the front door.

Marian: Too loudly.

Ellen: Using one of your feet because your arms are loaded.

Charlie: An' shouting up the stairs, shouting 'Hullo, there'. . . . Nothing. The house empty, the living room empty with a window open.

Marian: That windy autumn afternoon.

Charlie: And the curtains flying, flying.

[**Charlie** *picks up newspaper. The three ladies look into space. Tannoy comes on*]

Tannoy: Will Dr Green please report to the superintendent's office? Will Dr Green report to the superintendent's office immediately, please? Thank you.

Ellen: Charlie, you're reading the newspaper upside down.

Charlie: Wha'?

Ellen: Wrong way up – your *Daily Express*.

Charlie: I know what I'm doing.

Ellen: It's upside down.

Charlie: Mind your own business.

Ellen: Why are you reading the newspaper the wrong way round?

Charlie: [*muttering*] Bloody interfering with me. Women!

Ellen: I don't read the newspapers – too much gloom and doom. I've had enough catastrophe in my own life without reading that stuff. My interest in life is me.

Charlie: I always read the *Daily Express* upside down. I know what I'm doing.

Ellen: Biddy, did I tell you how my second husband got decapitated?

Biddy: Yes, an' we know it's all lies.

Charlie: I was enjoying this newspaper. You women mess things up.

Ellen: He worked on a fairground.

Biddy: Lies!

Marian: You've told us, Ellen.

Ellen: My second husband. On one of those machines that take you high up then whirl you round. There was this crane contraption. . . . His head got taken off, zoom, clean as a whistle.

[**Biddy** *cowers in her chair and puts her hands over her ears.* **Ellen** *goes closer to her, telling* **Biddy** *who doesn't want to hear.*]
And there he was strapped into the whirling seat minus head. Round and round his body went, just the blood pouring up through his torn neck.

Charlie: *Please*, you trying to make me puke?

Ellen: He was strapped in good. And they didn't stop the music for such a long time.

Marian: [*quietly*] Poor Ellen.

Ellen: Do you want to hear what happened to Hiram, my third husband?

Charlie: No!

Ellen: Okay so he was only a bum window-washer – and he was real slow at it too – but at least Hiram wanted kids which none of my other fellers did. He was only fifty-some but he had no spunk in him. They did a slide of his semen.

Marian: You've told us before, Ellen.

Ellen: Christ, his count was zero. Listen, Marian, I'd have had a different life if I'd had a child. Someone I could cherish. I wouldn't have bin so lonely. You know something? Narcissus didn't drown of self-love. Don't let them give you that stuff, kid. Narcissus drowned because he was so goddam lonely.

Biddy: [*mischievously*] You've got Jesus. How can she be lonely when she's got Jesus?

Ellen: You mocking me? You're so stupid and *you* are mocking *me*. You fat cow. You smell of ostrich's piss.

Biddy: You dung-ridden, poxed –

Ellen: Why you're dirty! You don't clean yourself! If you lay down with the dogs you'd get up with the fleas. Too bad Christ had to die for rats like you.

Charlie: [*shouting*] Ladies, ladies, *please*.

Marian: He's right. You two are always fighting.

Charlie: Can I have some tranquillity, a halcyon moment or two while I peruse this newspaper? Thank you.

[**Ellen** *giggles.* **Charlie** *growls, crushes his newspaper, then exits*]

Ellen: He's attractive when he's masterful. He's a horny little bugger.

[*Pause*]

Biddy: [*sadly*] It's years, years since I had a man.

[*Lights down*]

Scene Three

The superintendent's office. *The door is open. The phone is ringing. Enter* **Mr X.** *eating crisps. He stares at the phone. He takes a chair, puts it near the desk and stares intently at it as he eats crisps. Enter* **Pythagoras**. *He sits down in the superintendent's chair. Then he picks up a newspaper and ignores the phone.*

X: Shall I answer it?

Pythagoras: Better not.

X: It's getting on my nerves.

[**Pythagoras** *brings his arm over as if bowling at cricket. When his index finger is pointing at the phone it immediately stops ringing.* **X.** *eats crisps unconcernedly*]

You're on form. Bet you could read my thoughts today. Why am I in Dr Aquillus's office?

Pythagoras: Because you want to see Dr Aquillus.

X: [*seriously*] You *are* on form.

Pythagoras: And you're going to complain to him that you feel dead inside like you always do – that your intestines are made of glass.

X: True.

Pythagoras: Sometimes I can only bend a few knives or swords, stop clocks, and instigate a bit of thunder.

But today I feel I could raise the dead with an aurora borealis thrown in.

X: You'll be good at the concert tonight.

Pythagoras: When it comes to magic, Exy, things sometimes get out of hand, know what I mean? Once I had a ventriloquist's doll – I'm a pretty good ventriloquist too – but one night – it was at Porthcawl Pavilion – one night, I wasn't saying a word and the damned doll started talking on its own.

X: Sometimes I feel I'm just a puppet.

Pythagoras: I know that feeling.

X: That your words aren't your own? [*pause*] If I had your gifts I'd do so much good in the world. I'd bring down the bullies. Make lightning strike tyrants. I'd make rain fall in India. Stop floods with a secret incantation. Make crooked limbs straight with a touch. Make the old younger and the young happy. That's what I'd do.

[*Enter superintendent,* **Dr Aquillus**]

Pythagoras: [*laughing*] No use, Exy, I've tried. Moral profundity is an antidote to magic.

Aquillus: Perhaps God discovered that. Tsk, tsk, neither of you should barge into my office without an appointment. Besides you're Dr Green's patients, not mine.

Pythagoras: I have no confidence in Dr Green. His soul is so polluted.

Aquillus: Soul! What's the soul made of? Phlogiston? Ha, ha, ha.

Pythagoras: Xenophanes mocked me as you do, doctor. I had told him the soul of a man could migrate to a dog. Well, even as I speak now, Xenophanes is tethered to a drainpipe in an empty terraced street and is barking, barking.

Aquillus: Hmm. Dr Green with his interest in the occult should be fascinated by all that. But he tells me that apart from your recent medical history, he knows very little about you as you'll only talk about some imaginary life you led in ancient Samos and Croton.

Pythagoras: Green knows nothing about me.

X: [*brightly*] And we know very little about Dr Green.

Aquillus: If you were less taciturn about recent events —

Pythagoras: In Croton I gained more respect by saying little than others did by saying much.

Aquillus: Let us keep to this century. You used to have headaches in thundery weather when you were a small boy. You knew when thunder and lightning would occur.

Pythagoras: Right.

Aquillus: But later you began to think you could control the weather, could bring on thunder with a hey presto.

Pythagoras: That's what Dr Green told you?

Aquillus: At seventeen, you began to think you had extraordinary powers.

X: He has. Pythagoras is a miracle worker. He is in the company of Moses and Jesus.

Pythagoras: Why drag Moses and Jesus into it?

Aquillus: You became interested in following the profession of stage illusionist.

Pythagoras: I was apprenticed. I learnt my trade. Hypnotism. Ventriloquism. And I mastered the fraudulent gadgets. The quickness of the hand that deceives — but that's another thing. More to the point I began to recall more of the way I'd lived in Samos and Croton. And something I can't comprehend

29

would occasionally possess me and I'd become an instrument for it.

X: My bowels are made of glass.

Aquillus: Yes, yes.

X: I feel dead inside.

Aquillus: We'll talk about that later. As a matter of fact I want you to volunteer for the demonstration.

X: No! Definitely not.

Aquillus: Why not?

X: Definitely, definitely, definitely not.

[**Mr X** *begins to exit*]

Aquillus: Don't be alarmed, there's nothing to it.

[*Exit* **Mr X**]

X: [*off*] You're not going to exploit me.

Aquillus: [*shaking head*] Like you, he lives in the suburbs of punishment. But you – *you* feel inspired.

Pythagoras: I do see the correspondence of disparate things. That *is* inspiration. I know, too, the secret of irrationality, and I have the gift of approximate, prophetic insight.

Aquillus: Approximate?

Pythagoras: It's like a smell. I can't always be sure. If I told you of my other powers you'd poke fun at me.

Aquillus: No.

Pythagoras: If I told you I have power over animals, over poisonous snakes even, if I told you I could communicate with the souls inhabiting animals – even that parrot there – you'd think I was but a Greek shaman, or more likely that I was deluded and that these claims simply are symptoms of a schizoid personality. You're right. I have such a temperament. So had Isaac Newton, so had Einstein, and indeed they, too, had brief nervous breakdowns.

Aquillus: You don't think that because of your . . . breakdown . . . you imagine that you are Pythagoras?

Pythagoras: No, it is because I'm Pythagoras restored to this discordant century that I've had a breakdown.

Aquillus: Last year you had a partial gastrectomy because of a duodenal ulcer.

Pythagoras: I have a scar to prove it.

Aquillus: That ulcer gave you hell. It punished you. The operation too was a form of punishment.

Pythagoras: So?

Aquillus: Two years ago you admitted to piercing pains in the calves. Three years ago your right lung leaked air. That was painful. You've lived in the suburbs of punishment because you feel guilty.

Pythagoras: Sometimes when I can accurately foretell future events I do feel guilty. I admit that. As if I were a voyeur. As if I looked into a private room where a man is crying and a woman screaming. Of course, sometimes my ability to prophesy has been more ordinary. For instance, I know what horse will win the Derby next week.

Aquillus: [*chuckling*] I gotta horse.

Pythagoras: You're laughing at me again.

Aquillus: I'm sorry. Tell me something more significant. Is your mother alive, Pythagoras?

Pythagoras: Prince Monolulu by one and a half lengths.

Aquillus: Are you married? Tell me that.

Pythagoras: [*eyes closed*] Something in me is out of harmony.

Aquillus: [*loud*] Why won't you tell us anything important about yourself?

Pythagoras: [*opening eyes*] In Samos I had a slave Zalmaxis. I gave him his liberty, and he became a friend.

Aquillus: Oh no, no!

Pythagoras: My father, a Phoenician by birth, was a gem engraver and –

Tannoy: Will Dr Aquillus and Dr Green please come to D Wing immediately? Will Dr Aquillus and Dr Green proceed to D wing? Thank you.

Pythagoras: I can't really talk to you. You have no religious intuitions. Don't you know – outside that window is not just a gravel pathway winding between green lawns and high trees. It is revelation. Whichever way you look is revelation.

[*Pause*]

Aquillus: I'm keeping the students waiting.

[**Aquillus** *begins to exit*]

That horse. Prince Monolulu. Is there such a horse?

Pythagoras: Yes.

Aquillus: Ur, hm. What odds?

Pythagoras: [*smiling*] Twenty-five to one.

Aquillus: Mmm. Prince Monolulu.

[*Exit* **Dr Aquillus. Pythagoras** *bowls as in cricket to point finally at the phone which immediately rings.* **Pythagoras** *at once picks up receiver*]

Pythagoras: [*yelling*] Wrong number!

[*He swiftly replaces the phone, then raises his right hand upwards, fingers parted in the mystical position, and straightaway there is a lightning flash followed by a crack of thunder.* **Pythagoras** *is about to leave when he observes* **Dr Aquillus's** *white coat which he now tries on*]

Perhaps I should take over, try to cure them, and form a brotherhood.

32

[He is about to take off white coat when **Ken Kennedy**, *a young reporter, enters]*

Kennedy: Dr Aquillus?

Pythagoras: *[turning]* Mmm?

Kennedy: I wonder if you could spare me a few minutes?

Pythagoras: I'm not –

Kennedy: Sorry to barge into your office like this. I'm from *The Record*. I just want to give the concert a write-up. I believe my predecessor did so on the last occasion. I hope you don't mind, doctor. I did phone but I got no reply.

Pythagoras: That phone's out of order. Struck by lightning, probably.

Kennedy: Ha, ha, ha, struck by lightning! *[He hands* **Pythagoras** *his card]* Ken Kennedy. Everybody calls me Ken. I suppose the concert is therapeutic for the patients?

Pythagoras: Or for the doctors.

Kennedy: Ha, ha, for the doctors! I hear there's going to be a poetry reading and madrigals and you have an ex-stage magician.

Pythagoras: Yes, I'm the main ... I mean Pythagoras, one of our patients, is the main attraction. He's an extraordinary magician and this year we have prevailed upon him to give us a treat. He'll bring down the house, ha, ha, ha.

Kennedy: Pythagoras?

Pythagoras: Yes, a native of Samos who believes in the table of ten opposites, that ten is the sum of the first four numbers, that ten is the most perfect number, that the square on the hypotenuse of a right-angled triangle is equal to the sum of the squares on the other two sides and so forth and so on.

Kennedy: Bloody mad, eh?

Pythagoras: Mr Kennedy, many people say if Jesus came back they'd lock him up in a place like this.

Kennedy: I dare say.

Pythagoras: Anyway, Pythagoras won't be here long. He just has selective amnesia, that's all. He has forgotten certain small things. For instance, he's not absolutely sure whether he is, at present, married.

Kennedy: Small things! Ha, ha, ha. Doctor, you're a card. If he was married, he'd know all right. [*Pause*] I've been married four months and four days.

Pythagoras: Theano, oh Theano, dear one.

Kennedy: Wassat?

Pythagoras: Have you heard of the Orphic priesthood? Pythagoras learnt much in Egypt. A very knowledgeable man! Tonight, I'm quite sure he'll astound the audience. I can just picture the end of his act.

Kennedy: How do you mean?

Pythagoras: Pythagoras leaves the stage and still they are clapping. When he returns they clap even louder. The clapping seems as if it will never cease. He is bowing. He takes off one glove, they are clapping. He leaves the stage and they are clapping. The stage is empty and some are standing. The stage is empty and some are leaving. The stage is empty and some are clapping. The stage is empty and few are clapping. The stage is empty and the clapping ceases. The stage is empty and the seats are empty.

[*Pause*]

Kennedy: Doctor, that's a very odd description. Anybody could tell you're not an ordinary doctor. One can always tell a psychiatrist.

Pythagoras: You flatter me. All the doctors here agree that Pythagoras is truly a mystery man.

Kennedy: I expect a few certified patients are.

Pythagoras: Mmm. You probably don't appreciate the nature of true magic.

Kennedy: As a doctor, you don't believe in magic, do you doctor?

Pythagoras: The Hippocratic Corpus – though nowadays no doctor may read its seventy books – still informs the spirit of modern medicine in so far as it emphasises the importance of facts and data and the hesitating possibility of generalizing from the particular. Hence if all – shall we say – observed unicorns are white doctors would assume that unicorns are white invariably, do you follow? They wouldn't be able to recognize a black unicorn as a unicorn.

Kennedy: Unicorns don't exist.

Pythagoras: That's it! You've got the nub of the problem.

Kennedy: I have?

Pythagoras: Yes, very smartly.

Kennedy: Thank you.

Pythagoras: As you would be the first to agree, and as some bright poet has said: 'Unicorns don't exist because they have better things to do!' But the magician has to persuade a unicorn that what it is doing is so very boring that it may as well exist at least for a few seconds.

Kennedy: Ha, ha, ha, doctor you *are* a card, definitely. Yeh, so what you're saying, figuratively speaking, is that this patient Pythagoras can persuade unicorns?

[**Pythagoras** *closes his eyes, smiles smugly and perceptibly nods*]

Kennedy: [*mumbling*] Pythagoras. 'Mystery Man Of The Cedars.' [*louder*] Quite a good headline.

Pythagoras: Why not?

Kennedy: 'Searing Truths Of The Insane'. Ye-es, the editor may wear it. I'll get a photographer. Is Pythagoras photogenic?

Pythagoras: Oh, well. [*chuckles modestly*]

Kennedy: I won't be long. I have my bike outside.

Pythagoras: Wait a minute.

Kennedy: Won't be a jiff. Leave it with me, doctor.

[*Exit* **Kennedy** *in a hurry*]

Pythagoras: [*calling*] Mr Kennedy, Pythagoras believes in the transmigration of souls and in the beautiful order of things.

[**Pythagoras** *takes off the white coat, then gazes at the parrot*]

Pythagoras: Well, what do you think of that, parrot? Speak parrot. The soul of our grandam might haply inhabit a bird.

[*He brings up arms slowly above his head*]

I said, speak parrot. I, Pythagoras, command you to speak.

[**Pythagoras** *raises his arms further. His hands above his head touch*]

Parrot: Thou . . . shalt . . . not . . . eat . . . beans.

[*A great crash of thunder.* **Pythagoras** *ducks as if to take cover. Lights down.*]

Scene Four

[**The common room. Ellen, Biddy, Marian**]

Biddy: Christians take their hats off to pray. Jews put them on. Christians put shoes on to visit a church, Moslems at a mosque take them off. Just depends what team you support. May just as well be a follower of Pythagoras.

[*Pause*]

Ellen: I don't know what the opposite to an orgasm is – but that's what I get when I argue with you.

[*Enter* **Charlie** *right. Half running, his trousers rolled up above his knees.*]

Charlie: Ladies, ladies, ladies, do you like my legs?

[*Pause*]

Marian: Hairy.

Charlie: What do you think of them, Ellen?

Ellen: Well, they're all right *individually*.

[*Enter* **Mr X** *left followed by Arthur who stands in the background.*]

X: I'm not going, not going. NOT GOING.

Charlie: What's the matter?

X: He wants me to be the exhibit this morning. It's so demeaning.

Charlie: You're right. It's humiliating.

X: I feel I'm made of glass. I feel . . . feel dead. I am dead – and this is hell.

Biddy: Give me your hand, Mr X.

[**Mr X** *puts his hands over his face and they all look at each other*]

Biddy: Exy.

X: Yes.

Biddy: You're always saying you feel dead.

X: I am dead. I've known for years.

Ellen: How do you mean?

X: That time years ago when I was so small.

Ellen: What?

X: When I was small ... my father came into the room and he just didn't notice me.

Ellen: Aw hell, baby – often my daddy never noticed me either when I was a kid. Yeah, my father was stinkin' drunk mosta the time.

X: Here I am, I called to my father. He looked left at the flowers in a vase, he looked right at the lampshade. Here, here, I said – joyfully – because I thought he was just teasing me, just playing a game.

Marian: And wasn't he?

X: Here, here, Dad. But he walked past me as if I were elsewhere. This way, this way, I said loudly, not knowing now whether to laugh or cry. He looked upward at the crack in the ceiling. He looked downward at the pattern in the carpet.

Biddy: No, no, that way, *that* way.

X: And I thought – what chill pretences, especially when his face turned solemn as if he were about to utter the prayer for the dead.

Marian: Oh, no.

Ellen: Poor kid.

X: But it was when he looked around the room sadly and then knocked off the light closing the door behind him. . . .

Marian: Leaving you in the darkness?

Biddy: Then you *knew*.

X: Yes. And I'm not going to tell all that to ... *strangers*.

[*Enter* **Pythagoras**]

Charlie: Why should any of us be exhibited? We're not guinea pigs. Am I right, Pythagoras?

Pythagoras: Right.

Charlie: Why should we be exploited?

Biddy: Quite right.

Charlie: I have an idea. First, do you all agree the superintendent is an evil dictator like Poly ... Poly ... ?

Pythagoras: Polycrates.

Charlie: Exactly. Listen to me, all of you.

[**Charlie** *climbs on to a chair*]

Ellen: He's so horny.

Charlie: [*brandishing a water-pistol*] See this revolver? Who's with me?

Marian: That's just a water pistol.

Ellen: It's not, it's not. I'm with you, bud. We'll kill him.

Biddy: Me too.

Pythagoras: We're all with you.

X: Yes, yes.

Charlie: What about Arthur?

Marian: He hardly says a word except marmite.

Charlie: Get him by the throat and choke an answer outa him.

[**Arthur** *backs away as they stare at him*]

Arthur: [*screaming*] Mar-mite.

Pythagoras: Leave him alone. He won't give you away. He won't speak. The rest of you. Raise your right hands to swear your allegiance to Charlie.

[**Ellen, X and Biddy** *raise their right hands*]

All of you. I, Pythagoras command you.

[*First* **Marian** *then* **Arthur** *hesitantly raise their hands. There is a great shout followed by cries of*

'Speech Charlie', 'Nice one, Charlie', 'Atta boy, Charlie'.
Charlie *swells with pride and pleasure.*]

Charlie: Friends, countrymen, you with question marks in your spines, you with hunches and guesses, betcher a quid, a fiver, every dollar you've got, ten per cent, Barclays Bank, National Provincial, Middle and Leg.

Biddy and Ellen: Hear hear.

Marian: Easy, Charlie. Take it easy, Charlie.

[**Charlie** *suddenly twists his neck, is suddenly vulnerable and querulous.*]

Charlie: Something won't leave my mind, something like the red beak of a black swan.

[*Hearing this, they all stand quiet but when* **Charlie** *resumes his speech there are cries of 'Bravo', 'Hear, hear', 'Dead right'. Indeed during the rest of* **Charlie's** *speech there are cries occasionally from the others of 'Hallelujah' etc. as at a negro spiritual meeting. Even Marian joins in finally.*]

Charlie: They twist everything. They put it across *you*, the people. They put *you* in a hospital and call it The Cedars. They put *you* in a slum and call it Sycamore Drive. And what is this so-called Sycamore Drive? One pub, a free house – and a betting shop and a sweet shop and a row of terraced houses with no front gardens, no trees, no sycamores. A bit of a garage maybe and the only colour in the street a bit of an oilpool in the forecourt. And they call *this*, Sycamore Drive. It makes me puke.

All: [*clapping*] Hear, hear.

Charlie: Sycamore Drive, my arse. I went to that Free House and I had to pay for my beer. Went to a local restaurant and ordered Bombay Duck. What did I get? Dried fish.

All: Dried fish.

Charlie: That's what they do. Twist everything. A

public school is not for the public. A private in the army has no privacy; a family butcher doesn't butcher the family. Order Toad in the Hole and what do *you*, the people, get?

All: [*shouting*] Quite right. Hear, hear.

Ellen: Isn't he horny? Isn't he just darlin'?

Charlie: I promise you – when I take over, when the superintendent is buried near the thornbush – or the goldfish pool – I promise you, I swear, I swear, – no more demonstrations.

All: Hurrah, hurrah.

Charlie: I promise you no more prying medical students.

All: Hurrah.

Charlie: No more rancid butter, no more stewed tea, no more burnt toast, no more rice pudding, no more school custard. I promise you . . . *dignity*.

All: Hurrah, hurrah.

Charlie: I promise you . . . ev-er-y-thing.

[*Great cheering and hubbub. Enter* **Dr Bruce Green** *in a white coat. They fall silent raggedly.*]

Green: Good morning, Pythagoras. Oh, put that water pistol away, Charlie. Mr X, come with me, please.

X: Not me.

Green: It's all right. No need to worry.

Biddy: I'll come with you, Exy.

[**Biddy** *takes his hand and* **Dr Green** *nods and smiles.*]

Green: That's right. Meanwhile, I think you ought to rehearse the madrigals for tonight. Will you see to that, Charlie?

Charlie: Rely on me, Dr Green.

41

Green: I'm surprised at you, Marian.

[*Exit* **Green** *with* **X** *and* **Biddy** *right*]

Pythagoras: I'll change that pistol into a real revolver.

[**Pythagoras** *then takes a deep breath and shouts a long sentence in a foreign language that sounds like Greek*]

Charlie: It's all Greek to me. All right, let's 'ave you. First madrigal. By the right one, er two, er three. Move sharp, move sharp.

[*But* **Arthur** *exits right.* **Charlie** *half chases after him waving gun but as he does so* **Marian** *and* **Ellen** *exit left and he rushes back*]

Come back, come back.

Pythagoras: Let them go. I'll see to everything.

Charlie: What?

Pythagoras: I'm in charge again.

Charlie: *I* am. Well, I am, aren't I?

[*Pause*]

With your permission, of course.

[*Pause*]

Have you really changed this into a proper revolver?

Pythagoras: Yes.

Charlie: With bullets in it?

Pythagoras: Of course.

Charlie: And I could kill you?

Pythagoras: Certainly.

Charlie: [*pointing gun*] Aren't you afraid?

Pythagoras: Alas, no. My soul is too impure. Death would mean only another reincarnation not the final annihilation of self.

Charlie: We could give it a try.

[**Pythagoras** *shouts out something dramatic and loud in Greek again*]

Were those your last words?

Pythagoras: [*shakes head sadly*] Just turned that revolver back into a water pistol, that's all.

[*As* **Charlie** *looks at the gun, puzzled,* **Pythagoras** *exits.* **Charlie***, putting left finger in left ear and closing his eyes as if expecting a big bang, fires gun into the air. Water comes out. Lights down.*]

Scene Five

[Lights up. We are inside **the lecture theatre** *of The Cedars. Students are sitting in the first row of the audience and are facing a lectern with a chair each side of it. The medical students are talking amongst themselves but become silent with the entry of* **Dr Green** *and* **Nurse Grey**]

Green: My name is Dr Green. Welcome to those of you who have not visited The Cedars before. I think this morning some of you have come from Westminster Hospital. Anyway, our superintendent will be here shortly with his patients. But before this morning's demonstration may I make a few announcements. Every *other* year at The Cedars we have our *annual* concert, ha ha. This concert by the patients is to take place tonight at eight p.m. and you are all cordially invited. There will be madrigals and poems. Also one of our patients who, in better times, was a stage magician known as Pythagoras Smith, will also perform.

[*Enter* **Dr Aquillus** *with* **Biddy** *and* **Mr X. Nurse Grey** *directs* **Biddy** *to a chair left.* **X** *sits in chair right. Initially* **Dr Aquillus** *talks quietly to* **Dr Green.**]

Aquillus: Thank you, Bruce, for holding the fort. Have you told them about the concert?

Green: Yes, indeed. I'm going into London now to see that chap who used to be Pythagoras's agent. I'll be back in good time for the concert.

Aquillus: Good. Fine.

[*Exit* **Dr Green**]

Ladies and gentlemen, today I'm going to demonstrate these two patients. Bridget, who is known here affectionately as Biddy. . . .

[**Biddy** *moves her head a little, acknowledging the students*]

Her obesity is partly due to natural gluttony but partly the result of insulin therapy. . . . My second patient calls himself Mr X and has done so since he was cited in a divorce case.

[*The students laugh.* **Mr X** *does not mind but smiles benignly.*]

Aquillus: Others call him Exy.

X: [*mumbling*] I'm done in.

Aquillus: Mmmm? Do you want to address the students?

X: I'm dead beat.

Aquillus: Speak up, please.

X: I'm dead.

Biddy: [*suddenly rising to her feet*] I should be released. I get depressed sometimes, I even cry sometimes, but that does not make me . . . crazy. I get depressed because I haven't a man here. Frankly, I'm sexually deprived. That's all that's wrong with me. If they released me I might meet a man who excited me, who was interested in me. If I could have a proper relationship with a man I respected my small depression would be over, I assure you.

Aquillus: [*protectively, putting his arm around her*] Thank you. Thank you for your remarks.

[**Biddy** *sits down*]

Aquillus: Well, you must agree that what she says *sounds* reasonable. However, before we return to Biddy –

Student: Can we ask questions, sir?

Aquillus: After the demonstration, certainly. But please let me proceed. Allow me to invite Mr X. to address you. Come forward here, please.

X: Me?

Aquillus: Please. Thank you. I wonder if you would kindly tell these students how you spent your day yesterday?

X: On Thursday?

Aquillus: Yes.

X: I sat in the common room for eight hours.

Aquillus: Er, huh.

X: I drank eleven cups of coffee.

Aquillus: Yes.

X: I stared at the one stain in the ceiling.

Aquillus: Notice the obsessional tone to these comments – *eleven* cups of coffee, *eight* hours in the common room, *one* stain in the ceiling.

X: It looks like Africa upside down.

Aquillus: You stared at the stain that looks like Africa – and afterwards, what?

X: I reclined on the sofa. I put my hands behind my head and spat up at that stain on the ceiling.

Aquillus: Trying to score a bull's eye?

X: Yes. I spat up three times.

Aquillus: *Three* times.

X: Yes. I missed each time.

Biddy: It was raining on Thursday. It was too wet to go out.

X: There was nothing else to do. I counted twelve flies around the electric bulb. I spat up again at the stain three times. Twice, I missed. Then I dozed off. That was Thursday.

Aquillus: And today?

X: Today I'm dead.

Aquillus: Dead, did you say?

Biddy: No, no, no.

[**Biddy** *has risen from her chair and quickly* **Nurse Grey** *goes to her and gently settles her back in the chair*]

Aquillus: You're complaining of being dead?

X: Yes. I *am* dead and this is Hell.

Aquillus: I see. Take off your jacket, Mr X.

X: My jacket?

Aquillus: Yes, take it off, please.

[**Mr X** *takes his jacket off and puts it behind chair*]

That's it. Now roll up your right sleeve to show me your forearm. Nurse Grey, have you a needle?

Nurse: Yes, Dr Aquillus.

Biddy: No, no – don't, don't.

[**Aquillus** *takes needle*]

Aquillus: Tell me, Mr X, do dead men bleed?

X: [*gaily*] Of course not.

Aquillus: And you're dead?

X: Yes.

[**Aquillus** *scratches* **X's** *forearm*]

Biddy: [*turning away*] I can't stand the sight of blood.

46

Aquillus: Just a thin trickle. Deal with it, Nurse.

X: That just goes to prove. . . .

Aquillus: Yes?

X: That just goes to prove that dead men do bleed.

[*The students laugh*]

Aquillus: [*pointing to one of them*] Hoadley – what mental process have you just seen demonstrated?

Student: Rationalization, sir.

Aquillus: Quite right. An individual committed to a false premise will rationalize rather than give up his original belief. Delusion has to be reinforced by apparently logical argument. Mr X, would you mind sitting down now? Biddy, will you bring up your chair here, please? Nurse, give Mr X some water.

X: [*smiling happily*] I would like a glass of water.

Biddy: Shall I face them, Dr Aquillus?

Aquillus: Please. Now just tell them about your past – about what happened to you before you came to The Cedars.

[**Biddy** *opens her mouth, closes it again*]

Go on, dear.

X: They call me X because I'm an ex-person, an ex-human being. So I'm dead.

[*Again* **Biddy** *tries to speak but says nothing*]

Aquillus: She'll begin very soon. We'll just have to be patient.

[**Biddy** *begins to sob and cry. The students look upset. Then there is a cry of 'Stop it. Stop this demonstration.' It is* **Pythagoras** *shouting as he enters right*]

Pythagoras: [*in ringing tones*] Cease.

Aquillus: [*smiling*] Ah, our ex-stage magician. It seems we have a third patient.

Pythagoras: [*to students*] I'm more than a mere magician though I do have psychokinetic powers.

Aquillus: In this sultry June weather Pythagoras sometimes feels he can cause thunder and lightning.

X: Give us some thunder now, Pythagoras.

Pythagoras: When I was a small boy I used to suffer excruciating headaches in thundery weather. I always knew when it was going to lightning and thunder.

X: Please, Pythagoras.

Pythagoras: All right. One summer when I was sixteen I found that if I held the fingers of my left hand in this mystical way, then uplifted my left arm to the sky like this – watch me. One, two, three – I shall count to ten – four, five, six, seven, eight, nine, ten.

[*There is a flash of lightning. The students all talk at once. Then over the hubbub is the sound of thunder*]

X: [*nodding happily*] Told you so.

Pythagoras: [*looking at his watch*] In five minutes time exactly the nurse there will collapse.

Aquillus: Now, now, that's enough. [*to students*] You're all impressed by that coincidence?

Student: Well, it was uncanny, sir.

Aquillus: The feeling of something being uncanny occurs when what we have hitherto regarded as imaginary appears before us in reality. Uncanny is not quite the right word.

Biddy: When Pythagoras is around things happen.

Pythagoras: [*boasting*] A couple of years ago I visited Sicily and naturally Mount Etna erupted.

Aquillus: Naturally.

Pythagoras: You can be sarcastic. And I can't, of

course, be fully understood by these students either. When I say supernatural agencies work through me I know it sounds mad. Yet I am their agent and what happens exceeds human understanding – like that lightning flash you all witnessed.

[*Pause*]

Normally a man in a factory thinks of his domestic problems, is preoccupied. He does not hear the clanging of metal all about him nor the buzz of a bluebottle on a lathe. But if he opened his soul as mine is open then he'd hear everything. He'd hear the harmony of the spheres and he'd see the invisible.

Student: Have you seen a ghost, sir?

Pythagoras: A ghost?

Student: Yes.

Pythagoras: No, I have not seen a ghost.

Student: Ah.

Pythagoras: But I have smelt one.

[**Students** *laugh*]

Pythagoras: You modern students. You don't realize how privileged you are. In Croton, when I gave my lectures and demonstrations to the kousmatics and neophytes I stood concealed behind a curtain. But now, I suppose, you'd like some more thunder?

Students: Yes.
More thunder.
We want thunder.

Pythagoras: Very well. But you know whenever you hear a thunderclap you should all touch the earth as a remembrance of the creation of the universe. [*To* **Dr Aquillus**] To really believe, people like you must doubt first.

[**Pythagoras** *again holds his fingers as before and brings his arm higher into the air as he counts*]

One two three four five six seven eight nine ten.

[*Nothing happens.* **Pythagoras** *is dismayed*]

Aquillus: Surprise surprise, no thunder, no lightning, nothing. Ha, ha, ha – you students all look so disappointed, ha, ha, ha.

Pythagoras: [*shouting*] Stop laughing, Dr Aquillus!

Aquillus: I'm not laughing at you, Pythagoras, ha, ha, ha.

Pythagoras: You idiot quack, you won't be laughing tonight.

Aquillus: Quite right, I'm not laughing, the students aren't laughing.

Pythagoras: Don't patronize me. I promise these students that at the concert tonight I shall make a helluva lightning flash. There will be a thunderbolt. Beforehand I shall offer libations to the gods – offerings of oak leaves to Zeus, laurel to Apollo, rose to Aphrodite, vine to Dionysus. I shall sprinkle lustrations of sea-water from a golden vessel because the sea was the first to come into existence and gold is a most beautiful thing. And at nine o'clock exactly, on the stroke of nine – that number which symbolizes justice and retaliation – the superintendent here of The Cedars will have a coronary and *die*.

[**Nurse Grey** *now moans slightly and swoons to the ground in a faint. At once* **Dr Aquillus** *goes over to her*]

Student: He prophesied she'd collapse.

Aquillus: It's all right, Nurse. You'll be all right. His extravagant talk frightened her, that's all. There, there, she's reviving. Stand back, Biddy.

[**Dr Aquillus** *is taking her pulse. Everybody seems stupified except* **Pythagoras** *who ostentatiously looks* *at his wrist watch and nods his head triumphantly. Lights down as* **Nurse** *revives*]

[*End of Act One*]

Act Two

Scene One

[**The grounds. Pythagoras** *and* **Nurse Grey** *are sitting on a park bench.* **Pythagoras** *has his eyes closed.* **Nurse Grey** *is reading a paperback.* **Arthur** *left stage is staring into space. Noise of birds twittering*]

Arthur: I'll sing.

Nurse: [*still reading book*] In an hour or two when the concert begins.

Arthur: Now.

[*Pause*]

Nurse: At the concert. Quite right.

Arthur: Now.

[*Pause*]

Arthur: [*sings*] Oh, Shenandoah, I love your daughter, away you rolling river. Oh, Shenandoah.... [*He stops*]

Nurse: [*who has looked up to listen*] That was nice. Go on.

Arthur: No.

Nurse: I like that song, Shenandoah.

[**Arthur** *stares into space. The Nurse reads her book again. A pause*]

Pythagoras: Nurse, that novel's no good. Let me recommend the last and greatest book in Ovid's *Metamorphosis*.

Arthur: [*sings*] Ye banks and braes o' Bonnie Doon, how can ye bloom sae fresh and fair, how can ye chant ye little bird and I sae weary, fu' of care. Thou'lt break my heart. . . .

Nurse: Don't stop. Why stop?

[**Arthur** *stares into space*]

Pythagoras: Do you think the superintendent a compassionate man, Nurse?

Nurse: Yes, of course I do. Of course he is. He's a fine man. I like Dr Aquillus. A fine, fine man.

Pythagoras: Why?

Nurse: Why? Well, he's kind, you know that. Very punctilious and concerned for you all. He is a model of restraint. Her character is without blemish. She is a wonderful person.

Pythagoras: *She* is?

Nurse: Certainly is.

Pythagoras: The superintendent?

Nurse: Certainly. The way he looks at you . . . candidly. It calms you. He calms the patients. He has a firm but tranquillizing personality. You know he will not let you down. She would never let you down. She's so loyal.

Pythagoras: Who?

Nurse: The superintendent.

[**Arthur**, *listening to all this, decides he's had enough and exits quickly singing*]

Arthur: [*sings*] Oh, Shenandoah, *etc.*

Nurse: Where are you going?

Arthur: [*off singing*] Away you rolling river.

Nurse: Oh, dear. I forgot to let him have the new tablets.

[**Nurse** *exits*]

Nurse: [*off*] Wait for me, wait for me.

Arthur: [*off singing*] Oh, Shenandoah, I love your daughter *etc.*

Pythagoras: [*chants*] Gold bring me bread, black bring me water, five stones in the air, three on the back of my hand, two in the dust, now you know me, gold bring back our son to us, black bring home our daughter. Red hides the blood, green hides the slaughter, five –

[*Stops chanting, looks to right and stands up. Enter* **Kennedy**]

Kennedy: I've been looking for you everywhere. The editor wasn't keen on my idea. Also the Minister for Education is speaking at the Town Hall at eight-thirty and the other reporter – oh well, I can't stay for much of the concert, Dr Aquillus.

Pythagoras: What happened to the photographer?

Kennedy: Drat him.

Pythagoras: What?

Kennedy: Drat him.

Pythagoras: What do you mean, drat him?

Kennedy: Drat him. [*pause*] What's that building?

Pythagoras: D wing.

Kennedy: [*uneasily*] Is it safe wandering around?

Pythagoras: I'm most disappointed you won't see our great magician at work.

Kennedy: Don't worry, I'll give you all a good write-up. It's peaceful here. Peaceful but lonely.

Pythagoras: Lonely?

Kennedy: Quite. Outside these walls, in the city, it's lonely too. As a reporter I come across – you'd be surprised. . . . The other week – you know Marks and Spencers?

Pythagoras: Uh, huh.

Kennedy: A man was clinging to a ledge on the fifth floor, right up high, threatening to jump off. The ambulance screeched in, the fire engines, the police, a helluva palaver, and hundreds, *thousands*, over an hour or so gathered in the square all looking up at him.

Pythagoras: I can picture it.

Kennedy: He came down on his own at sunset. No more commotion, no problem. Came down meekly. I asked him, mister, I said, why did you climb up there, why did you cause all that trouble, and he said, for the first time in years, he said, everyone seemed concerned about me. Then he took an apple out of his pocket and munched it and the police took him away.

Pythagoras: So?

Kennedy: So I think it's wonderful. There was this man watching the people peering up at him, pointing. Don't you see – he didn't feel on his own any more. He felt all of them willing him not to jump, not to jump. *Don't jump.* So he came down . . . and ate an apple.

Pythagoras: You're a sentimentalist.

Kennedy: No.

Pythagoras: Bet half of them were thinking: jump, you bastard. Jump and be quick about it because I've got to get home, I've got to go to the office, I've got a phone call to make, got a letter to write, so hurry up mate, jump so I can see you beat your brains out on the pavement.

Kennedy: No, no – you've got it wrong. I'm willing to – who's that?

Pythagoras: Mmm?

Kennedy: Now there goes a lonely man. As a reporter you get to know human nature.

[*Enter* **Dr Aquillus** *who stops to admire some flowers*]

Pythagoras: That man's dangerous. He has delusions of grandeur. He thinks he's the superintendent, he thinks he's me.

Kennedy: The way he walks you can tell.

Pythagoras: Worse, he attacked another patient last week. He's an animal.

Kennedy: For no reason?

Pythagoras: No reason at all, grabbed him by the throat.

Kennedy: Christ, he looks dangerous. You can see from his face.

Pythagoras: He's most mean too. Stingy.

Aquillus: Hello, there. Taking a breather before the concert?

Pythagoras: Yes indeed.

Aquillus: Excuse me – you're from D wing?

Kennedy: I'm from the *Record*. Just came over to have a word with the superintendent about the concert.

Aquillus: Nobody told us.

[**Kennedy** *is searching in his pockets*]

Lost something?

Kennedy: Just looking for my cigarettes. I don't seem to have a ... very sorry I seem to have left ... Have you a fag, Dr Aquillus?

Aquillus: I don't smoke.

Kennedy: What about you, Dr Aquillus?

Aquillus: I don't smoke.

[*Pause. Sound of a bird whistling*]

Pythagoras: I used to take the poppy seed and bark of the squill but I've never smoked.

Kennedy: Poppyseeds?

Pythagoras: Oh, ha, ha, ha, that was thousands of years ago.

Aquillus: I use opium sometimes. Yesterday, as a matter of fact.

Kennedy: [*to* **Pythagoras**] Do you have many drug addicts here?

Aquillus: When I look around me I say, thank God for drugs.

Kennedy: Thank God for drugs?

Aquillus: I don't know what I'd do without them. I do my best, you know. I've not killed too many people over the years.

[*Exit* **Pythagoras** *to left quickly. At first* **Kennedy**, *who is staring at* **Dr Aquillus** *with horror does not notice* **Pythagoras's** *departure*]

Kennedy: Where's. . . ? Hey, come back. What did he slope off like that for?

Aquillus: I really don't know. Er, what was I saying?

Kennedy: You said you hadn't killed too many people.

Aquillus: Ha, ha, ha, no. Well. I presume you want me to talk about our research programme? Or do you want to stick to the concert?

Kennedy: I have to be at the Town Hall before eight-thirty.

Aquillus: Do you know what Machiavelli said?

Kennedy: Mac who?

Aquillus: He said whoever wishes to organize a State

and establish its laws must presuppose that all men are mad. I agree. Now periodically men are heaven-sent to guide the destinies of others. I ask myself if I am such a man.

Kennedy: What does Dr Aquillus say?

Aquillus: I say I am – in all modesty.

Kennedy: [*rises*] I think we ought – [*looks at his watch*] I think we ought to join the others.

Aquillus: [*rising*] Damn it all – look at that. People putting the lights on in D wing and it isn't dark yet.

[*They begin to exit right*]

Kennedy: What is your opinion of Pythagoras – your magician patient? Is he also an astrologist?

Aquillus: He believes he's the original Pythagoras, you know. Born in Samos at five-thirty.

Kennedy: P.m.?

Aquillus: [*stops walking*] BC.

Kennedy: Oh, sorry.

Aquillus: The original Pythagoras believed in reincar-nation. Our patient believes he can, at times, see into the future. He thinks I'm going to fall down dead with a coronary at nine o'clock tonight, mmm, mmm.

[*They continue to exit right*]

Kennedy: You ought to tell that to Dr Aquillus.

[**Superintendent** *grabs* **Kennedy** *by the arm. Again they stop walking. They stand momentarily extreme right stage*]

Aquillus: You think I ought to tell that to Dr Aquillus?

Kennedy: Yes.

Aquillus: I should tell him of this unpleasant prophecy?

Kennedy: Why, yes.

Aquillus: What did you say your name was?

Kennedy: [*gulping*] Kennedy.

Aquillus: [*gently*] Which . . . one?

Kennedy: Mmm?

Aquillus: Do you like it in D wing?

Kennedy: I think we should go straight away to Dr Aquillus.

Aquillus: How are you sleeping?

Kennedy: With my wife.

[**Aquillus** *nods and lets go* **Kennedy's** *arm. They resume walking and exit*]

Aquillus: [*off*] My dear boy, are you very depressed? Come to my office and I'll prescribe something.

Scene Two

[**The Common Room. Biddy, Ellen** *and* **Pythagoras**]

Pythagoras: I never said that. I believe the physical world is dualistic. Cosmic evil has to exist – otherwise there'd be no perfect harmony.

Ellen: Yeh, yeh, but you suggested Christ wanted to lam outa Jerusalem when they wanted to shaft him.

Biddy: Well, Jesus was causing riots. Jesus claimed he was the Son of God.

Ellen: He *was* the Son of God. I may be a poor, childless, defenceless woman but I *know*.

[*Enter* **Mr X**]

Pythagoras: And I'm Pythagoras. You believe Jesus was resurrected but you don't –

Ellen: You're a pagan. Betcher go in for all kinda swinish sacrifices.

59

Pythagoras: No, I always preached against bloo‹ sacrifices. My followers in Croton offered honey an‹ barley on the altars of the gods.

Biddy: There you are. That's very civilized.

Ellen: Look, lover boy, why don't you eat beans? Tel me that, go on.

Pythagoras: You know, I shouldn't divulge the reasor for this but I'll tell you. [*Pause*] I once carried ou‹ an experiment. I put beans in a pot, then burie‹ them in mud. When later I dug them up, the bean‹ had taken the shape of human embryos.

Ellen: Ha, ha, ha, what a load of shit ha, ha, ha, av go get your hair cut. He's just a punk heathen.

Biddy: An' you're a Jesus freak.

Ellen: Oh, hooey. His religion is so far out you can'‹ argue with him in a rational way.

[*Enter* **Charlie**]

X: You should show him more respect. Pythagoras wa‹ the first man to recognize the world was a sphere.

Pythagoras: Two and a half thousand years ago – ‹ hate to boast – I was philosopher, mathematiciar and magician.

Ellen: You shoulda specialized, buster. You won't get anywhere unless you specialize.

Pythagoras: That's what Heraclitus said; 'polymathy' – the learning of many things – 'does not teach understanding otherwise it would have taught Hesiod and Pythagoras, Xenophanes and Hecataeus.'

Ellen: Ain't that what I said?

Pythagoras: Difficult to wear both the white coat of science *and* the magician's purple one. You have to be . . . *very great.* [*pause*]
White coat and purple coat
   a sleeve from both he sews.

That white is always stained with blood
  that purple by the rose.

Biddy: Very good. Arthur'd like that.

Pythagoras: And phantom rose and blood most real
  compose a hybrid style,
white coat and purple coat
  few men can reconcile.

White coat and purple coat
  can each be worn in turn,
but in the white a man will freeze
  and in the purple burn.

Biddy: He's better than Arthur.

Charlie: Hm, hm. You think you're a mathematician, too, eh?

K: Pythagoras is a mathematical genius.

Charlie: What's eighty-five times sixty-two times sixty six. Ha, ha, ha. Tell me that, go on. Ha, ha, ha. [*bullying*] I said eighty-five times sixty-two times sixty-six: go on, multiply, multiply, ha, ha, ha, ha, ha, ha.

[*Pause as* **Pythagoras** *closes his eyes*]

[*Pointing*] Mathematician eh? Ha, ha, ha. Ha, ha, ha. Ha, ha, ha.

Pythagoras: [*opening eyes*] Three hundred and forty-seven thousand, eight hundred and twenty.

[*Pause*]

Biddy: ha, ha, ha, ha, ha, ha.

Charlie: Wait a minute. Hang on. Let me write it down. What did you say? I wanna check.

Pythagoras: Three hundred and forty-seven thousand, eight hundred and twenty.

Charlie: Three ... Four ... Seven ... Eight ... Two

61

... Oh. OK, wait a minute. What did *I* say? What did I ask you to multiply?

Biddy: Eighty-five times sixty-four times sixty-six.

Pythagoras: No. Eighty-five times sixty-two times sixty-six.

Charlie: [*writing*] Eighty-five by sixty-two by sixty-six.

[**Charlie** *sits in chair extreme right stage and works out this sum*]

X: He'll be right. Did you know Cicero visited his tomb at Metapontum?

Ellen: Don't listen to all his stories. He's got the devil in him. Like the parrot in the superintendent's office.

X: Tell them what it was like in the middle of the sixth century, Pythagoras. Tell them what you believe in.

Pythagoras: I believe in the harmony of the opposites, in the transmigration of souls. I believe we should not eat flesh.

Ellen: What a faggot!

Pythagoras: I was interested in mathematics – but mathematics leads you to ask certain questions about the ultimate nature of reality.

Ellen: Crap.

X: He had disciples.

Pythagoras: I had good pupils. [*pause*] Alcmaeon – he was a good boy. He was the first to dissect animals. He discovered the optic nerve and the Eustachian tubes. An excellent pupil, Alcmaeon. Yes, Croton was a lively place, then. And, later, you know, in Athens Plato and his boys were much influenced by my teachings. Alas, Plato had a totalitarian sensibility.

Charlie: [*shouting*] He's right, he's right. Three hundred and forty seven thousand, eight hundred and twenty. Bloody marvel. What a fuckin' mathematician.

X: He never makes errors.

[*Exit* **Charlie** *right muttering*]

Pythagoras: Oh, I do. I did. My style was in the error.

Charlie: [*Off*] Fuckin' stupendous!

Pythagoras: I made mistakes, my pupils too. You see, there was a rift eventually. Some were capable of apprehending the scientific side of my teachings but neglected the ethical and magical side. On the other hand there were those who did not eat meat or beans, would not look in a mirror that hangs beside a light, and so on, but forgot the moral purpose of these restrictive rituals, or had no head for science.

Biddy: White coat and purple cloak few men can reconcile.

Pythagoras: Exactly. Sometimes, because of my pupils I was misunderstood. They wanted me to be semi-divine. There was so much fabrication and legend-mongering. One idiot babbled I had a golden thigh. No wonder that fool Zeno wrote a book against my teachings, and Heraclitus, the Riddler, that haughty, dark one, criticised me. [*Pause*] Now, excuse me, before dinner, I'm going to listen to Bach. I like his mathematical precision. And afterwards I shall let my soul ascend to the heavens in wordless adoration.

Ellen: You'll have to make it snappy, bud, it's nearly dinner time now.

Pythagoras: Don't forget at nine you will all witness the death of . . .

[*Enter* **Nurse Grey** *right*]
. . . of one who I now realize has the soul of the tyrant.

X: Polycrates?

Nurse: [*cheerfully*] Your daughter's here, Ellen.

Ellen: I have no daughter.

Biddy: What's she brought Dr Aquillus this time? Goldfish? Last time it was that speechless parrot.

Nurse: She's come to hear you sing the madrigals.

Ellen: Gloria?

Nurse: You may have dinner with her in the TV room, if you wish.

[*Enter* **Marian** *left*]

Ellen: Gloria's too busy in the pet shop to come and see me.

Biddy: I'd like a puppy. Couldn't she give me a little spaniel puppy?

Nurse: She's waiting for you in the main hall.

Ellen: The devil . . . the devil is in all her animals.

[*Exit* **Ellen**]

Nurse: Marian, the superintendent said you can leave next week.

Biddy: [*taking* **Marian's** *hand*] Oh, Marian, love.

Marian: That's wonderful.

Nurse: Monday, if you like.

Marian: I see Dr Green on Mondays. I'd like one more session with Dr Green.

Nurse: I understand. We'll say Tuesday, shall we?

Marian: That would be good.

[*There is a sound of a bell ringing*]

Biddy: I'm starving.

[*All except* **Pythagoras** *begin to exit right*]

Marian: [*desperate*] Wednesday, Nurse Grey. Wednesday afternoon. Could we leave it till then?

Nurse: [*off*] Of course. Of course, Marian. There's no hurry.

[**Pythagoras** *is now alone. He turns towards the radio and flings both arms towards it pointing with both index fingers. At once we hear Bach's violin concerto in E. Major.* **Pythagoras** *sits down and listens to the music with eyes closed. Slow lights down, music slowly fading*]

Scene Three

[**The superintendent's office. Kennedy** *and* **Dr Green** *are seated.* **Dr Aquillus** *is fixing a drink. The door of the parrot's cage is ajar and there is no sign of the parrot*]

Kennedy: He certainly confused me.

Aquillus: We all make mistakes.

Kennedy: A plausible character, Pythagoras.

Green: He convinced his agent. He really believes Pythagoras Smith is Pythagoras reincarnated. He still, each morning, as once instructed by Pythagoras, keeps his eyes closed and peers at the back of his eyelids. Then he recalls in detail the events of the day before so that he may judge his own conduct and rectify moral error. He's a weird agent.

[**Dr Aquillus** *has handed a drink to* **Kennedy** *who stares at it with dismay*]

Aquillus: Anything amiss?

Green: I think our guest would like a little more than that, Robert.

Aquillus: Oh, of course.

[*But* **Dr Aquillus** *does not offer any further drink to Kennedy*]

Apart from his agent you didn't see anybody else?

Green: I called on his former landlady.

Aquillus: Ah.

Green: No use. She's also trying to start a local Pythagorean Society. She herself does not eat beans. Goes about barefoot. Won't walk on the highway. Refuses to pick up anything that's fallen. She didn't think much of me. She said, 'All psychiatrists are mentally wounded.' Maybe she's right.

Aquillus: Rubbish! I think you yourself half believe your patient was born in the Island of Samos in 531 BC.

Kennedy: Ha, ha, ha, ha, ha, ha.

[**Dr Kennedy** *stops laughing when both doctors look at him unsmilingly*]

Aquillus: The concert must have started. I think we'd better go.

Green: Last week I gave some sodium amytal to Pythagoras intravenously, talking to him all the time about his childhood while he was in this medicated trance.

Kennedy: Why did you do that?

Aquillus: A psychiatrist has to have the patience of a cat.

Green: To discover things about his early childhood. When he spoke a most strange language I asked our linguist professor patient in D Wing to come over.

Aquillus: Kanellatos? He's too far gone.

Green: No. He told me it was ancient demotic Greek.

Aquillus: You believed him?

Green: He translated several of his remarks. Here they are.

[**Dr Green** *hands a piece of paper to* **Dr Aquillus**]

Aquillus: [*reads*] When I stroked the head of the white eagle it stretched its wings.

Kennedy: I bet, ha, ha, ha.

Aquillus: [*reads*] We must erect a cenotaph for those who break the rules and divulge the secrets of a lifetime. . . . Appollonius of Tyana is an imposter. [*Looks up*] Who's Appollonius?

Green: No idea.

Aquillus: [*handing paper back to* **Dr Green**] Well.

Kennedy: It's nonsense.

Aquillus: At best it has a sense of a dream. And I'd say the dream of poor drugged Kanellatos.

Green: I don't think so.

Aquillus: Oh, you Jungians are too credulous. It's a good job our patient cursed me, not you – or else I really do believe that at nine o'clock tonight you would expire. [*to* **Dr Kennedy**] Please excuse me, I must go to the concert. [*to* **Dr Green**] I forcefully suggest you join me soon and put that stupid mystical stuff behind you.

[*Exit* **Dr Aquillus.** **Dr Green** *fills up* **Kennedy's** *glass*]

Green: Allow me. Our superintendent is a great man, but cautious.

Kennedy: I don't think much of him as a psychiatrist, frankly.

Green: Why? He's very astute.

Kennedy: For a kick-off he has difficulty in differentiating the sane from the um – very sane.

Green: We all make mistakes, ha, ha, ha. Cheers!

Kennedy: Cheers!

Green: I made a very clever mistake once. One evening not long after I qualified as a doctor I'd drunk . . .

er, my fill, when I was called out to a middle-aged lady. It was when I was taking her pulse I realized I was a bit tanked up. I couldn't count properly and I said to myself, 'Mmm, a bit too much alcohol'. I must have said it out loud because my patient remarked, very impressed, 'That's very clever of you, doctor'. Ha, ha, ha – she was a *secret* drinker. She thought, ha, ha, ha, that I had caught her out.

Kennedy: Ye – es, but not being able to tell the difference between the sane and insane is, I'd say, a very worrying thing in a psychiatrist.

Green: I don't know. [*pause*] I mean, Dr Aquillus is a very kind man – very kind to me. Keeps me here despite my eccentricities, some of which, even to me seem almost pathological! Ha, ha, ha, I have many irrational anxieties.

[**Dr Green** *fills up glasses again*]

Kennedy: Cheers!

Green: Cheers!

Kennedy: What do you mean by irrational anxieties?

Green: Well, for instance, statistically speaking, there are very few air crashes, agreed?

Kennedy: Agreed.

Green: But do you know, when I'm in a plane about to land or to take off, I have a distinct feeling of unease.

Kennedy: Normality gone mad.

Green: What?

Kennedy: Well, Dr Aquillus has his eccentricities too.

Green: Certainly. No question.

Kennedy: For instance, not many people keep an empty cage in their office.

Green: Heavens! The parrot's gone.

[**Dr Green** *goes over to the cage*].

Kennedy: Oh. I thought an empty cage was supposed to be symbolic or something.

Green: [*bending*] There are some feathers here. I don't understand.

[**Dr Green** *rises and soon is peering over the other side of the desk*]

Kennedy: I've got this Town Hall thing to report at eight-thirty. [*Looks at his watch*] Drat.

Green: My God! Come here.

Kennedy: What is it?

[**Kennedy** *joins* **Dr Green**. *They stare at something hidden behind the desk*]

Green: It's beheaded.

Kennedy: That's really sick.

Green: Five months ago somebody beheaded a cat. It was outside my door. We never found out who did it. There was an unsigned note. It said 'Too many mouths to feed'.

Kennedy: Ha, ha, ha, too many mouths, ha, ha, no, no, you're right, it's not funny. All that parrot's blood, uch. That's the trouble with my job. You run into all kinds of unpredictable things. You can't afford to be too sensitive.

Green: That parrot being slaughtered . . .

[**Dr Green** *pours out drinks*]

. . . it's very odd.

Kennedy: Yeh, you're always on the outside, know what I mean? More disasters than celebrations. It's a glimpse of a funeral, oh, I dunno, of strangers wearing black, mourning a stranger. 'Parrot shock at The Cedars', yes, I can see that headline.

Green: It's almost like a sacrifice.

[They both drink from their glasses as lights fade and out].

Scene Four

[The concert. The curtain is down. In front of it, **Charlie**, **Ellen**, **Biddy**, **Arthur**, **Mr X** *and* **Nurse Grey** *smile and bow]*

Nurse: *[stepping forward]* Thank you. Our last madrigal this evening is a most difficult one – but I hope it will amuse you. It is by the fifteenth-century composer, Banchaeri. Ladies and gentlemen, Contra-punto Bestiali.

[At the end of the madrigal they bow and **Dr Aquillus** *enters right applauding. They all exit right to join audience, but* **Dr Aquillus** *stops* **Arthur** *and keeps him by his side]*

Aquillus: Thank you. Most of you know our own bard, Arthur Haines, who before he made his, er . . . home here had a book of poems published by Faber. It was called, I think, *Marmite and Other Poems*. For some years he's written very little verse. But tonight he has agreed to read us a new poem. Please keep your hands in the applauding position for this poem is going to be short!

[While **Dr Aquillus** *was speaking* **Arthur** *turned his back to the audience]*

No, no, no. Good boy. As I was about to –

Arthur: Self.

Aquillus: What?

Arthur: Self. *[yells] Self* . . . by . . . me.

Aquillus: Quite.

Arthur: [*recites*] Elf . . . himself . . . herself . . . thyself . . . myself . . . shelf.

[**Arthur** *begins to exit left.* **Aquillus** *chases after him and brings him back stage centre*]

Aquillus: I must say your skill surprises me. That poem of yours encapsulates most economically not only the spirit of narcissism but the complicated reciprocity between ego-libido and object-libido. Yes, in a logically unassailable way, he differentiates the energy of the ego-instinct from the ego-libido, and the ego-libido from the object-libido. So succinctly, I'm startled. His poem, 'Self', began, you recall, with the word Elf. Elf, no less. A creature that does not exist – any more than do the souls in Dante's *Inferno* or the apparitions in Shakespeare! I do really –

Arthur: [*sings*] Thou'lt break my heart, thou warbling bird, *etc.*

[*Exit* **Arthur** *singing left*]

Aquillus: Oh, well. It is time in any case for the next act. Excuse me. Excuse me.

[*Sound of drums. Curtain rises.* **Dr Aquillus** *exits left to sit in the audience with students and rest of the cast. In Spotlight,* **Pythagoras**, *right, in top hat and purple cloak and* **Marian** *wearing the appropriate clothes of a magician's assistant. To the left are three Windsor chairs. On one of them, now in shadow, is a ventriloquist's doll*]

Pythagoras: My Lord and Lady Mayor, meat-eaters, fish-eaters, all of you who are by murder clothed and by murder fed, pray silence for –

Marian: Pythagoras! Magician extraordinary! [*whispers*] Pythagoras, Pythagoras, Pythagoras.

Pythagoras: [*chants*] Gold bring me bread, black bring me water, five stones in the air, three on the back of my hand, two in the dust, now you know me. Gold bring back our son to us, black bring home our daughter.

Marian: [*whispering*] Pythagoras, Pythagoras, Pythagoras, Pythagoras.

[**Marian** *continues to whisper 'Pythagoras' using sometimes a different tone in her voice, e.g. one of surprise or delight. She is also rhythmically upraising her arms and flapping her hands in a rather comical way*]

Pythagoras: [*chanting*] Red hides the blood, green hides the slaughter, five knives in the air, three in the back of the hand, two in the dust, now you know me, red bring back our son to us, green bring home our daughter.

Marian: [*whispering*] Pythagoras, Pythagoras, Pythagoras.

Pythagoras: Ha, ha, ha. You like her? I'll put her up for auction.

Marian: [*squeaking*] Pythagoras! [*Whispering*] Pythagoras, Pythagoras.

Pythagoras: How much for her beautiful head, how much for her beautiful legs? How much for her red buried heart? C'mon, bid, bid.

Marian: [*whispering*] Pythagoras etc.

Pythagoras: I'll give you a hammer of ebony, nails of silver too, and a varnished plank of pine to hit the nails right through.

[**Marian** *gives a little scream*]

So bid, bid, bid. And going, going, gone, says the little pink worm. [*pause*] Now for some thunder.

[**Pythagoras** *throws both his hands in the air, cries out loudly something long and haunting in Greek. There is a pause. Instead of thunder* **Arthur** *is heard singing briefly off stage, 'Thou'lt break my heart!'*]

Pythagoras: [*conversationally*] Ladies and gentlemen. The practice of magic is an imprecise art. A bit hit and miss. Sometimes it's chicken but sometimes it's only feathers. Dark, pristine powers have to be coaxed from their arcane hiding places. And when ghosts are the colour of air we must all be supplicants. So please help me. When I say, Gold bring me bread, I want you to repeat that magical phrase. I say Gold bring me bread and you say Gold bring me bread. And so on. You follow? Good. [*Loud*] GOLD, BRING ME BREAD.

[*Pause*]

No, no, no, no, no. Don't be so self-conscious. Are you so over-bred and over-civilized? You're not at home now, you know. No slacking. You can do better than that. You *will* do better than that. [*Shouts*] Gold, bring me bread.

Cast, students and audience: Gold, bring me bread.

Pythagoras: Better. But in this free-enterprise society I see you need incentives. If you repeat what I say loud enough, then this beautiful, hypnotized puppet here will remove articles of her clothing, *phrase by phrase.* [*loud*] Gold, bring me bread.

Cast, students and audience: Gold, bring me bread.

[**Marian** *removes a bow from her hair*]

Pythagoras: Black, bring me water.

Cast, students and audience: Black, bring me water.

[*Psychodelic lights on* **Marian** *as she takes off both her shoes and removes bodice*]

Pythagoras: Wait a minute. Tease them a bit. What kind of a dame are you? One shoe at a time is enough. Don't rush it. Have you ever seen anyone so keen? Never mind. Now, loud please, loud. FIVE STONES IN THE AIR.

Cast, students and audience: Five stones in the air.

[**Marian** *removes skirt*]

Pythagoras: Now, let us see whether you are men or mice. THREE ON THE BACK OF MY HAND.

[*Enter* **Charlie** *from left running and holding a gun*]

Charlie: [*shouting*] Off with them, off with them.

[*Exit* **Marian** *right hastily, chased by* **Charlie** *who is firing gun.* **Pythagoras** *raises his hand to call for silence. He addresses the audience.*]

Pythagoras: You all look so disappointed. Let me remind you of the Greek proverb: when you've seen one tit, you've seen two. I recognize that snigger. It's the Archbishop of Canterbury. What? Yes, I do need a new assistant. Now who – pardon? No . . . I don't know where he got hold of the gun.

[*Enter* **Biddy**]

Ah, Biddy. Thank you. Sit down there. Now we have one chair empty. I need one more volunteer, please. C'mon, c'mon. What about you? Ah. . . .

[*Enter* **Mr X**]

My old friend, I should have guessed.

X: Shall I sit there, Pythagoras?

Pythagoras: That's right. Biddy, you look sad. Ladies and gentlemen, you don't know the rage that lies behind the face of misery. Biddy, if you smile, I'll make something nice happen. Smile and close your eyes. Splendid. Think of something that you would like to happen *now*. Good. Good. All right, that's simple. For love is simple, am I correct, Exy?

X: Yes.

Pythagoras: Love lasts as long as there are two people, however silent the word.

X: [*rising*] Yes.

Pythagoras: Love is a small flame in a gunpowder factory.

74

*[**X** slowly walks towards **Biddy**]*

X: Yes.

Pythagoras: Love is like moonlight that makes even a slum beautiful. Love is a woman waiting at a night window,

*[**X** has taken **Biddy's** hand. She lifts his hand to her cheek, her eyes still closed]*

who stares down at an empty street of lamp posts. Ha, ha, ha! How sentimental I am. This one too – *[He points at the ventriloquist's doll]* don't you think he also wants to be loved? *[He picks up doll]* Doesn't he look familiar? Ladies and gentlemen, allow me to introduce to you . . .

*[He holds up the dummy to audience. The face of the dummy resembles that of **Dr Aquillus**. Lights all down now except on **Pythagoras** who speaks like a boxing referee]*

. . . my privilege. . . . On my right hand the Champion, DR ROBERT AQUILLUS, SUPERINTENDENT OF THE CEDARS.

Dummy: *[speaking with the taped voice of the superintendent]* I must say your skill surprises me. For you do not exist any more than do the souls in Dante's *Inferno* or the apparitions in Shakespeare. *[pause]* Also let me remind you of your promise. It's nearly nine o'clock, Pythagoras. Do you hear?

[There is a faint sound of a clock striking]

Pythagoras: *[taking a long needle from his cloak]* True, true. Ye-s. Six . . . seven . . . eight . . . NINE.

*[He plunges needle into doll's left chest from which oozes a red fluid. **Pythagoras** himself makes a very long strange noise before collapsing in slow motion]*

[strangulated] Polycrates.

*[**Dr Aquillus** rushes on stage followed by **Nurse Grey**. The audience has a quick picture of **Dr**

Aquillus *listening to* **Pythagoras's** *chest with a stethoscope while* **Nurse Grey** *supports his head.* **Mr X** *and* **Biddy** *in background watch anxiously. Lights down*]

Scene Five

[**Superintendent's office**, *six months later. The parrot's cage has been taken away. Distant sound of carol singers: 'Silent Night'. Outside it is snowing. Soon there is a murmur of voices.* **Dr Aquillus** *and* **Dr Green** *are approaching followed by* **Charlie**]

Charlie: [*calling off*] Dr Aquillus, Dr Aquillus wait for me. I want to consult you too, Dr Green.

Aquillus: [*off*] Not now, Charlie.

Charlie: [*off*] I told Ellen I'm agin Paul, Peter, The Apostles, The Martyrs, The Confessors, the Evangelists.

Green: [*off*] Charlie!

Charlie: I prefer goddesses to gods.

[*Enter* **Dr Green** *and* **Dr Aquillus** *followed by* **Charlie** *who is holding a bottle of wine*]

Green: What are you trying to say?

Charlie: I'm trying to say I don't like this place. Especially now, at Christmas. I don't like the company. I want to ask for a transfer.

[*Carol singers stop singing*]

Green: Where to?

Charlie: [*whining*] I want to be put in the women's ward.

Aquillus: [*looking at wrist watch*] Where's Pythagoras?

Charlie: This is my good-bye present for him.

Aquillus: Where did you get that?

Charlie: I've 'ad it six months. Just before the concert, last summer, Pythagoras told me he could change water into wine. So I got 'old of an empty bottle and I filled it up with a sample.

Green: Sample?

Charlie: Yes . . . a sample.

Green: I don't follow.

Charlie: My own. . . . Crikey, you're thick. Dr Green, the doctor-patient relationship is based on the assumption that the doctor has superior knowledge to the patient. Anyway, Pythagoras held it up to the light. Turned the bottle round nine times, uttered some Greek stuff, and lo . . . and *lo* as they say in the Bible. Lo!

Aquillus: You tried some of it?

Charlie: Took a glass. Didn't care for it. Wrong vintage. Would you like a drop yourself, Dr Aquillus?

Aquillus: Oh, no.

Charlie: Don't blame you. It tastes like piss.

[**Charlie** *makes for door taking bottle with him*]

Yes . . . say good-bye to Pythagoras for me. [*At the door*] Another thing. It's six months since Ellen decapitated that parrot and you haven't done a bloody thing. [*shouts*] I demand a trial.

[*Exit* **Charlie**]

Aquillus: My God, he's getting difficult.

Green: I reduced his dose of chlorpromazine.

Charlie: [*off*] At the Old Bailey. Justice! Justice!

Aquillus: I'm sure Pythagoras won't remember changing that urine into wine.

Green: Ha, ha, ha, wrong vintage.

Aquillus: You know when you finish your paper you should send it to *New Psychiatry*. Pythagoras was such an odd case.

Green: Strange how he improved so quickly after he collapsed at the concert.

Aquillus: The ECT helped.

Green: I hope we aren't being too precipitate, letting him out for Christmas.

Aquillus: I don't think so. In your paper will you cite any parallel cases?

Green: I intend to refer to that woman at Duke University in North Carolina who had telepathic powers.

Aquillus: Mmm?

Green: It so happened she also had thyrotoxicosis. When they operated on her thyroid, curing her, she simultaneously lost her telepathic gifts.

Aquillus: Good heavens. That authentic?

Green: Oh, yes.

[*Enter* **Nurse Grey** *and* **Pythagoras** *who looks reduced, ordinary. He is carrying a suitcase*]

Nurse: Here he is, Dr Aquillus. All neat and shining and ready to say good-bye.

Pythagoras: And to say thank you.

Nurse: [*to Aquillus*] I'll just see if his wife has arrived at the main hall. I'll phone across as soon as I know.

Aquillus: Fine.

[*Exit* **Nurse**]

Green: Ready to face the cold, cold snow, Tony?

Pythagoras: Yes.

Aquillus: Best not to go back to stage work. I advise a routine job.

Green: He's taking a temporary clerk's job in the New Year. It's settled.

Aquillus: That should not be too demanding. Yes, that's a good bet – better than my bet ha ha ha on Prince Honolulu last June, remember?

Pythagoras: Monolulu.

Aquillus: Quite right, Monolulu.

Pythagoras: I feel as if I've been absent from my own life.

Aquillus: I understand. You read too much about Pythagoras, thought too much about Pythagoras, dreamed about Pythagoras, asleep and awake. So much so, you, Tony Smith, became . . . ill.

Pythagoras: One thing, doctor, before I go.

Green: Yes.

Pythagoras: Some of the other patients – Biddy, for instance – told me some lines I wrote about a white coat and a purple cloak.

Green: So?

Pythagoras: *I can't write poetry, Dr Green.* And Charlie reckons I did fantastic sums in fifteen seconds flat – *but I'm not particularly good at mathematics.*

Aquillus: Charlie's hardly a reliable witness, Tony. Besides, we all have powers which we do not generally call upon, powers which we hardly know we own. There's nothing preternatural in that.

Pythagoras: I suppose so. Yes, it's absurd, you're right – like thinking, like thinking I could make that phone ring.

[**Pythagoras** *points at the phone and it rings. The superintendent hesitates, then chuckles and picks up the receiver*]

Aquillus: Yes. Yes, thank you, Nurse. Tell his wife he's coming over right away.

[**Dr Aquillus** *puts down phone and laughs heartily.*
Dr Green *joins in laughter. But* **Pythagoras** *puts
down suitcase and sits down, evidently disturbed*]

Aquillus: It was just a coincidence . . . that phone.

Green: Are you all right, Pythagoras?

Aquillus: Don't call him Pythagoras. His name is Tony
Smith.

Pythagoras: I'll just sit down a minute. I'll be all
right in a sec.

[*The snow outside descends across the window. Very
faint now the distant carol can be heard again. Lights
gradually down*]

Funland

1 The superintendent

With considerable poise
the superintendent
has been sitting for hours now
at the polished table

Outside the tall window
all manner of items
have been thundering down
boom boom stagily
the junk of heaven.

A harp with the nerves missing
the somewhat rusty
sheet iron wings of an angel
a small bent tubular hoop
still flickering flickering
like fluorescent lighting
when first switched on
Elijah's burnt-out chariot
various other religious hardware
and to cap it all
you may not believe this
a red Edwardian pillar box.

My atheist uncle has been standing
in the corner wrathfully.
Fat Blondie in her pink
transparent nightdress
has been kneeling
on the brown linoleum.

And for some queer reason
our American guest yells
from time to time Mari-*an*
if they give you chewing gum
. . . . CHEW.

Meanwhile the superintendent
a cautious man usually
inclined for instance
to smile in millimetres
has begun to take a great risk.

Calm as usual
masterful as usual
he is drawing the plans of the void
working out its classical proportions.

2 Anybody here seen any Thracians?

The tall handsome man
whom the superintendent
has nicknamed Pythagoras
asked fat Blondie
as she reclined strategically
under the cherry blossom
to join his Society.

The day after that
despite initial fleerings
my uncle also agreed.
The day following another hundred.
Two more weeks everyone
had signed on the dotted line.

There are very few rules.
Members promise to abstain
from swallowing beans. They promise
not to pick up what has fallen
never to stir a fire with an iron
never to eat the heart of animals
never to walk on motorways
never to look in a mirror
that hangs beside a light.
All of us are happy with the rules.

But Pythagoras is not happy.
He wanted to found
a Society not a Religion
and a Society he says
washing his hands with moonlight
in a silver bowl
has to be exclusive.
Therefore someone must be banned.
Who? Who? Tell us Pythagoras.
The Thracians yes the Thracians.

But there are no Thracians among us.
We look left and right wondering
who of us could be a secret Thracian
wondering
who of us would say
with the voice of insurrection
I love you
not in a bullet proof room
and not with his eyes closed.

Pythagoras also maintains
that Thracians have blue hair and red eyes.
Now all day we loiter near the gates
hoping to encounter someone of this description
so that what is now a Religion
can triumphantly become a Society.

3 The summer conference

On grassy lawns
modern black-garbed priests
and scientists in long white coats
confer and dally.

Soon the superintendent will begin
his arcane disquisition
on the new bizarre secret weapon.
(Pssst–the earwigs of R.A.F. Odiham)
Meanwhile I–suprise surprise–
observe something rather remarkable
over there.

Nobody else sees it (near the thornbush)
the coffin rising out of the ground
the old smelly magician himself no less
rising out of the coffin.

He gathers about him his mothy purple cloak.

Daft and drunk with spells
he smiles lopsidedly.
His feet munch on gravel.

He is coming he is coming here
(Hi brighteyes! Hiya brighteyes!)
he is waving that unconvincing
wand he bought in Woolworths.
He has dipped it in a luminous
low-grade oil pool.
Bored with his own act he shouts
JEHOVAH ONE BAAL NIL

Then a lightning flash ha ha
a bit of a rumble of thunder.
Nothing much you understand.
Why should the aged peacock
stretch his wings?

At once the scientists take off
the priests hurry up
into the sky. They zoom.
They free-wheel high over rooftops
playing guitars;
they perform exquisite
figures of 8
but the old mediocre reprobate
merely shrinks them
then returns to his smelly coffin.
Slowly winking he pulls down the lid
slowly the coffin sinks into the ground.
(Bye brighteyes! Arrivederci brighteyes!)

I wave. I blink.
The thunder has cleared
the summer afternoon is vacated.
As if a cannon had been fired
doves and crows
circle the abandoned green lawns.

4 The poetry reading

Coughing and echo of echoes.
A lofty resonant public place.
It is the assembly hall.
Wooden chairs on wooden planks.
Suddenly he enters suddenly
a hush but for the small
distraction of one chair
squeaking in torment on a plank
then his voice unnatural.

He is an underground vatic poet.
His purple plastic coat is enchanting.
Indeed he is chanting
'Fu-er-uck Fu-er-uck'
with spiritual concentration.
Most of us laugh
because the others are laughing
most of us clap
because the others are clapping.

In the Interval out of focus
in the foyer Mr Poet signs his books.
My atheist uncle asseverates
that opus you read Fuck Fuck–
a most affecting and effective
social protest Mr Poet.

In the ladies' corner though
Marian eyeing the bard
maintains he is a real
sexual messiah
that his poem was not an expletive
but an incitement.
Fat Blondie cannot cease from crying.
She thinks his poem so nostalgic.

Meanwhile the superintendent asks
Mr Poet what is a poem?
The first words Eve spoke to Adam?
The last words Adam spoke to Eve
as they slouched from Paradise?

Mr Poet trembles
he whistles
he shakes his head Oi Oi.
As if his legs were under water
he lifts up and down in slow motion
up and down his heavy feet
he rubs the blood vessels in his eyes
he punches with a steady rhythm
his forehead
and then at last
there is the sound of gritty clockwork
the sound of a great whirring.

He is trying to say something.

His sputum is ostentatious
his voice comes through the long ago.

After the interval
the hall clatters raggedly into silence.
Somewhere else distant
a great black bell is beating
the sound of despair
and then is still.
Cu-er-unt Cu-er-unt chants the poet.
We applaud politely
wonder whether he is telling or asking.
The poet retires a trifle ill.
We can all see that he requires air.

5 Visiting day

The superintendent told us
that last summer on vacation
he saw a blind poet
reading Homer
on a Greek mountainside.

As a result my atheist uncle
has fitted black lenses
into his spectacles.
They are so opaque
he cannot see through them.
He walks around with a white stick.
We shout Copycat Copycat.

In reply his mouth utters
I don't want to see I can't bear to see
any more junk dropping down.
Meanwhile visitors of different sizes
in circumspect clothes in small groups
are departing from the great lawns–
though one alone lags behind and is waving.

She in that blue orgone dress waving
reminds me how I wrote a letter once.
'Love read this though it has little meaning
for by reading this you give me meaning'
I wrote or think I wrote or meant to write
and receiving no reply I heard
the silence.
Now I see a stranger waving.

October evenings are so moody.
A light has gone on
in the superintendent's office.
There are rumours that next week
all of us will be issued
with black specs.

Maybe yes maybe no.

But now the gates have closed
now under the huge unleafy trees
there is nobody.
Father father there is no-one.
We are only middle-aged.
There are too many ghosts already.
We remain behind like evergreens.

6 Autumn in Funland

These blue autumn days
we turn on the water taps.
Morse knockings in the pipes
dark pythagorean
interpretations.

The more we know
the more we journey into ignorance.

All day mysterious aeroplanes
fly over
leaving theurgic vapour trails
dishevelled by the wind
horizontal chalky lines
from some secret script
announcing names perhaps
of those about to die?

Downstairs the superintendent
sullen as a ruined millionaire
says nothing does nothing
stares through the dust-flecked window.
He will not dress a wound even.
He cannot stop a child from crying.

Again at night
shafting through the dark
on the bedroom walls
a veneer wash of radium
remarkably disguised
as simple moonlight.
My vertebral column
is turning into glass.

O remember
the atrocities of the Thracians.
They are deadly cunning.
Our water is polluted.
Our air is polluted.
Soon our orifices will bleed.

These black revolving nights
we are all funambulists.
The stars below us
the cerebellum disordered
we juggle on the edge of the earth
one foot on earth
one foot over the abyss.

7 Death of the superintendent

With considerable poise
in a darkening room
the superintendent sat immobile
for hours at the polished table.
His heart had stopped in the silence
between two beats.

Down with the Thracians.
Down with the Thracians
who think God has blue hair and red eyes.
Down with the bastard Thracians
who somehow killed our superintendent.

Yesterday the morning of the funeral
as instructed by Pythagoras
all members on waking kept their eyes closed
all stared at the blackness
in the back of their eyelids
all heard far away five ancient sounds fading.

Today it's very cold.
Fat Blondie stands inconsolable
in the middle of the goldfish pool.
She will not budge.
The musky waters have amputated her feet.
Both her eyes are crying simultaneously.
She holds her shoes in her right hand
and cries and cries.

Meantime our American guest tries
the sophistry of a song.
The only happiness we know she sings
is the happiness that's gone
and Mr Poet moans like a cello
that's most itself when most melancholy.

To all of this
my atheist uncle responds magnificently.
In his funeral black specs
he will be our new leader.
Look how spitting on his hands first
he climbs the flagpole.
Wild at the very top he shouts
I AM IMMORTAL.

3 Lots of snow

First the skies losing height
then snow raging and the revolution bungled.
Afterwards in the silence
between two snowfalls
we deferred to our leader.
We are but shrubs not tall cedars.

Let Pythagoras be
an example to all Thracian spies
my tyrant uncle cried
retiring to the blackness inside
a fat Edwardian pillar box.

Who's next for the icepick?

Already the severed head of Pythagoras
transforms the flagpole
into a singularly
long white neck.

It has become a god that cannot see
how the sun drips its dilutions
on dumpy snowacres.

And I? I write a letter to someone nameless
in white ink on white paper
to an address unknown.
Oh love I write
surely love was no less
because less uttered or more accepted?

My bowels are made of glass.
The western skies try to rouge the snow.
I goosestep across this junk of heaven
to post my blank envelope.

Slowly night begins in the corner
where two walls meet.
The cold is on the crocus.
Snows mush and melt
and small lights fall from twigs.

Bright argus-eyed the thornbush.

Approaching the pillar box
I hear its slit of darkness screaming.

The end of Funland

Uncle stood behind me
when I read Mr Poet's poster
on the billiard cloth
of the noticeboard:
COME TO THE THORNBUSH TONIGHT
HEAR THE VOICES ENTANGLED IN IT
MERLIN'S
MESMER'S
ALL THE UNSTABLE MAGICIANS
YEH YEH
DR BOMBASTUS TOO
FULL SUPPORTING CAST.

Not me I said thank you no
I'm a rational man touch wood.
Mesmer is dead these many years
and his purple cloak in rags.

They are all dead replied uncle
don't you know yet
          all of them dead–
gone where they don't play billiards
haven't you heard the news?

And Elijah the meths drinker
what about Elijah I asked
who used to lie on a parkbench
in bearded sleep–he too?

Of course sneered uncle
smashed smashed years ago like the rest of them
gone with the ravens gone with the lightning.
Why else each springtime
with the opening of a door
no-one's there?

Now at the midnight ritual
we invoke Elijah Merlin Mesmer the best of them
gone with the ravens gone with the lightning
as we stand as usual in concentric circles
around the thornbush.
Something will happen tonight.

Next to me fat Blondie sobs.
Latterly she is much given to sobbing.
The more she sobs the more she suffers.

Suddenly above us
frightful insane
the full moon breaks free from a cloud
stares both ways
and the stars in their stalls tremble.

It enters the black arena aghast
at being seen and by what it can see.
It hoses cold fire over the crowd
over the snowacres of descending
unending slopes.

At last in the distance we hear
the transmigration of souls
like clarinets untranquil played by ghosts
that some fools think to be the wind.

Fat Blondie stops her crying
tilts her face towards me amazed
and holds my hand as if I too were dying.
For a moment I feel as clean as snow.

Do not be misled I say
sometimes Funland can be beautiful.
But she takes her hand away.

I can see right through her.
She has become luminous glass.
She is dreaming of the abyss.
We are all dreaming of the abyss
when we forget what we are dreaming of.

But now this so-called moonlight
is changing us all to glass.
We must disperse say goodbye.
We cannot see each other.
Goodbye Blondie goodbye uncle goodbye.

Footsteps in the snow
resume slowly up the slope.

They gave me chewing gum so I chewed.

Who's next for the icepick?

Tell me are we ice or are we glass?

Ask Abaris who stroked my gold thigh.

Fu-er-uck fu-er-uck.

Do not wake us. We may die.